"Stan Block's account of the suffering of the hu[...] I have never seen the matter put better."

Huston Smith, author of *The World's Religions* and *Why Religion Matters*

"I have suffered chronic back pain for sixteen years with a host of complications. Dr. Block's simple yet powerful methods did not completely stop the pain but rather rendered the pain a smaller and smaller portion of my reality. I exchanged the twin evils of goal-setting and self-loathing for healthy involvement in family, church, and work. This is not psychobabble. Its premise is new and revolutionary. You are *not* broken! You don't need fixing!"

Peter J. Sorensen, Ph.D., Associate Professor of English, Brigham Young University

"Dr. Block's bridging methods have given me new ways to help pitchers deal with adversity and prepare them for the major leagues."

Rafael Chaves, Pitching Coach, Tacoma Rainiers Baseball Club, AAA Affiliate of the Seattle Mariners

"Stanley Block's work moves towards the outer frontier of present-day wisdom, philosophy, and ontology by pointing out how we mortals severely handicap ourselves by unwitting submission to the unconscious dictates of the Identity System."

James S. Grotstein, M.D., Clinical Professor of Psychiatry, UCLA School of Medicine, and author of *Who Is the Dreamer Who Dreams the Dream?*

"Bridging and mapping will change our whole approach to teaching living skills to high-risk children."

Walter Beach, CEO, Amer-I-Can Program of New York

"Bridging is an inner practice of seeking wisdom and truth manifesting in an outer practice of compassion and loving kindness."

William D. Geoghegan, Ph.D., Professor Emeritus of Religion, Bowdoin College, and author of *Jung's Psychology as a Spiritual Practice and Way of Life: A Dialogue*

"Block's insights are having a major impact on pain and addiction patients, helping them to be open to change, reducing resistance to care, and avoiding relapses."

Stanley J. Evans, M.D., Board of Directors, Caron Foundation, and Clinical Assistant Professor of Psychiatry, University of Vermont Medical School

"The Identity System is a fundamental tool we teach our clients to use in their daily lives. It allows them to instantly tune in to the divine relationship with their Higher Power and defeat thoughts of shame and guilt. As clients learn how to bridge the Identity System, the risk of relapse is greatly diminished."

Gloria Boberg, Executive Director, Ark of Little Cottonwood, Sandy, Utah

"I have been waiting thirty years for someone to express spirituality in modern scientific terms."

Dennis Genpo Merzel, author of *The Eye That Never Sleeps* and *24/7 Dharma*

"This book leads the reader on a journey of self-discovery that involves a simple and speedy yet powerful and elegant process for letting go of worry and depressive inner dialogue."

Ann P. Hutton, Ph.D., APRN, Director of Psychiatric and Mental Health Nurse Practitioner Program, University of Utah College of Nursing

"Bridging has given me more time and energy. I now have the tools to serve my community."

Jules Harris, Ed.D., Consultant to Temple University Center for Social Policy and Community Development.

"With bridging, my energy, enthusiasm, and health have been better than any time in the last fifteen years. Since being certified in Identity System theory and technique, I have helped over one hundred women regain their innate vitality and overcome past traumas. Bridging is the secret to beauty, wisdom, and strength, 24/7."

Theresa McCormick, M.S., APRN, Psychotherapist, Salt Lake City

"Dr. Block's very simple method to deepen our personal faith and compassionate actions is truly a gift."

Reverend Roger H. Anderson, Pastor, Christ Lutheran Church, Los Angeles

"A new approach to good (Yetzer Tov) and evil (Yetzer Rah) well worth hearing, sharing, and using."

Rabbi Harry Z. Sky, Rabbi Emeritus, Temple Beth El, Portland, Maine

"Bridging and mapping are taught to my instructors to enable them to carry yoga practice into everyday life."

D'ana Baptiste, Founder, Centered City Yoga, Salt Lake City

"Our stress-management classes are more successful than ever with Dr. Block's methods."

Jonathan Josebachvili, M.A., Clinician, Department of Psychiatry, Kaiser Permanente, San Diego

"Bridging awareness practices, Identity System theory, and mind-body mapping have proven to be powerful tools for clients receiving treatment in our domestic-violence services."

Gary Baker, Executive Director, Cornerstone Counseling Center, Salt Lake City

"Stan Block gives us simple tools to overcome the fiction of our separateness from Truth or God."

Robert Tapp, Ph.D., Professor Emeritus of Humanities and Religious Studies, University of Minnesota

Come to Your Senses

Come to Your Senses

Demystifying the Mind-Body Connection

Stanley H. Block, M.D.

with Carolyn Bryant Block

BEYOND
WORDS
Publishing
I N C

Published by
Beyond Words Publishing, Inc.
20827 NW Cornell Road, Suite 500
Hillsboro, Oregon 97124
503-531-8700

The information contained in this book is intended to be educational. The author and publisher are in no way liable for any use or misuse of the information. The ideas, techniques, and suggestions in this book are not intended as a substitute for expert medical or mental-health professional diagnosis, advice, or treatment. If you are under the care of healthcare professionals, please consult with them before altering your treatment plan. All names and identifying information of individuals in this book have been disguised to protect their anonymity.

Editor: Laura Carlsmith and Julie Steigerwaldt
Managing editor: Sarabeth Blakey
Proofreader: Marvin Moore
Cover design: Jerry Soga
Composition: William H. Brunson Typography Services

Printed in the United States of America
Distributed to the book trade by Publishers Group West

Library of Congress Cataloging-in-Publication Data
Block, Stanley H.
    Come to your senses : demystifying the mind-body connection / Stanley H.
  Block with Carolyn Bryant Block.
      p. cm.
    Includes index.
    1. Identity (Psychology).   2. Mind and body.   I. Block, Carolyn Bryant.
  II. Title.

    BF697.B575   2005
    158.1—dc22

                                        2004029967

The corporate mission of Beyond Words Publishing, Inc:
  Inspire to Integrity

We appreciate all who have helped us to refine, implement, and document our findings about the Identity System. A special thank you is given to the thousands who have attended our workshops, classes, and individual sessions. Their transformed lives have made this book possible. *Come to Your Senses* is dedicated to those seeking to live life at its best.

C o n t e n t s

Introduction

The Discovery

"I treated him, God cured him."
—Ambroise Paré

In my forty-year career as a physician, psychiatrist, and psycho-analyst, I pondered the mysteries of healing. I believed that if we could discover the obstacles to healing—the ways we impede our natural healing processes—we could greatly reduce the toll of human suffering. We could liberate our inherent vitality to heal not only our physical lives but our emotional and spiritual lives as well. In pursuit of these goals, I began to look for a system within the human body that might be responsible for interfering with our natural healing.

We know that natural healing is our birthright. At this moment, as you read this page, cells in your body, damaged or dying as a part of everyday life, are being healed and rejuvenated. Similarly, as you take your next breath, numerous problems are being resolved deep within your brain. Just as your muscles natu-rally mend and recover following strenuous exertion, so your mind naturally heals from the stresses and strains of everyday life. Natural healing systems inherent to the human organism harmo-nize and bring balance at physical, mental, and spiritual levels, maintaining health throughout.

The human organism is a miraculous arrangement of inter-connected systems. The cardiovascular system regulates blood flow. In the heart, blood vessels and a vast neuroendocrine net-work deliver oxygenated blood to the brain, heart, muscles, and vital organs. The gastrointestinal system, consisting of the mouth, esophagus, stomach, small intestine, large intestine, and the rectum and metabolic organs such as the liver and pancreas, breaks down and metabolizes food. The central nervous system is like the CEO of the entire arrangement of systems, with its brain, brain stem, spinal cord, and peripheral systems, all of which are intricately orchestrated to direct the body and mind's activities and keep them healthy.

Nowhere in these recognized systems could I find an element that seemed to address the root of human dis-ease or unhappiness. Early in my career, as a theoretical physicist, I had been employed by General Dynamics as a guidance-system scientist, working on rockets and satellites, and as a research scientist for Rand Corporation, working on a neural net for adaptive behavior. The disciplined approach to identifying and solving systemic problems provided a framework for my quest. My faith in a higher power, beyond the conception of my limited mind, allowed me to persevere in spite of a series of failures. By a higher power, I mean that ineffable essence of your being, whether you call this essence God, Jesus, Allah, Buddha, Universal Consciousness, the Absolute, or Nothingness. I prefer the term *Source*. You can't be separated from this Source of life any more than a ray of light can be separated from its source. Yet, do you experience this connection during your daily activities? I didn't. I lacked a sense of well-being; no matter how successful I was, peace of mind eluded me, and I became determined to discover the hindrance that prevents us from experiencing a 24/7 connection to the Source of all goodness—and to the healing that is our birthright.

After several years, the answer arrived, not with a bang but with a hum. One evening, I was relaxing in the living room. All was quiet except for distant traffic sounds and the normal household sound of the refrigerator running. Suddenly the refrigerator hum stopped. A bit later, it started up. Yet the refrigerator had been running the entire time. I listened intently and noticed that whenever I had thoughts, the refrigerator hum faded. It suddenly occurred to me that my self-centered thoughts had shut off my ears! I began to notice that when I directed my attention back to the machine hum, I was calm. When I lost the sound, my mind was cluttered with thoughts, my body was tense, and my peripheral vision collapsed.

My own thoughts had triggered a collapse of my awareness! Suddenly it dawned on me: *The closing down of our awareness shuts us off from our essence.* With closed-down senses, we are separate from our Source and all existence. And it was the profoundly simple act of hearing a mundane sound that brought me "back to my senses."

As the weeks passed, I began to take more notice of my senses. I realized that I touched hundreds of objects each day but was unaware of how any of them really felt. I saw hundreds more sights and people but could not really say that I "saw" them. Like most of us, I often found myself driving home from work, arriving in my driveway, and not being able to recall one thing that I had seen on the journey home.

I had identified the problem—collapsed awareness; now I needed to discover what this "thing" is that contracts awareness and spoils our enjoyment of life. It was obvious to me that the act of thinking itself could not be the cause, because thinking is a natural function. I had discovered that I could still think and hear background sounds simultaneously. I ultimately found that only particular thoughts trigger our inability to experience our Source. When awareness expands, certain thoughts, but not others, trigger a system that collapses down awareness. For me, it meant that when I drove on the freeway, I would often miss my exit. When someone was talking to me, I did not always hear what he said. When I dressed in the morning, or walked, or exercised, I did not experience my movement. I didn't sense the myriad objects I touched. When the system, whatever it was, was "on," I was not functioning "on all cylinders." At that point, I had no name for this system that prevents us from experiencing our essence and from living our life at its best. And I had yet to discover what purpose it served.

More answers came, this time from the mouth of a babe.

One day, on a plane I sat behind a mother and her three-year-old daughter. I watched as they talked and related to a fellow who sat across the aisle from them. The mother was pleased with her daughter, who proudly said, "I'm Elizabeth," when the man said, "I'm Joe. Who are you?" They talked pleasantly, he kidded her, and she laughed. Continuing in this light vein, he started to call her Joe. She immediately corrected him: "I'm Elizabeth." Carrying the teasing further, he continued to refer to her as Joe. She soon became tense and fearful and started to cry. "I'm Elizabeth!" she screamed in frustration. Joe quickly stopped the kidding, and before the end of the flight, with her mother's comforting and urging, Elizabeth and Joe made up.

A light bulb went off in my head. The name "Elizabeth" was not only the *name* the little girl could be called but was also *who she thought she was*. When this identity was challenged, a whole system was activated. The system I had been searching for, the system that was the root of human dis-ease, stress, and unhappiness, was the *Identity System*! I found I could suddenly relate to Elizabeth's distress. Like her, when my identity (who I believed I was) was challenged, my Identity System was activated, producing anxiety, physical tension, impaired functioning, and contracted awareness.

In *Come to Your Senses*, I explore the human Identity System and how it disrupts our natural mind-body connection and restricts the awareness and healing of every human being on the planet. The book not only identifies the problem that keeps you and me from living our fullest life, but it also provides an easy and life-changing set of tools to circumvent your Identity System's manipulations. In twelve chapters you will learn how to map and recognize your Identity System's tricks and then how to rest your Identity System so you can function naturally and freely. Numerous examples from my workshops provide context and encouragement as you read about how to come back to your senses and live the full life you were meant to live.

The Identity System holds enormous power over all of us. Learning about it can unleash your endless, innate essence. My goal is to encourage you to use *Come to Your Senses* to experience for yourself an immediate, powerful, progressive, permanent, and positive life transformation. The shift in consciousness you will experience while reading *Come to Your Senses* is instantaneous, starting when you first create the simple maps that clearly show how your Identity System limits you and causes suffering.

With this transformation, your negative self-talk—whether it's "He doesn't love me," "I can't do this," "My back pain will never allow me to be active again," or "This will never turn out right"—will disappear into the vastness of your natural self. As you know, the power of positive thinking is short-lived. In this book, you won't learn how to "be" a certain way; instead, you will become aware of how to become *more* of who you truly are— more vital and more authentic. If currently you don't have time to enjoy and appreciate your life, the bridging practices you'll learn will expand the fullness of your life. If you can't relax your mind after a hard day, you'll learn how to settle your busy head. You will see that it is as easy to rest the mind as it is to rest the body. Examples ranging from individuals who struggle with pain, illness, addictions, and trauma to those seeking to improve performance illustrate the discussion throughout the book.

You are never too old for this kind of life-altering change. Jeanette, seventy-one years old, found her life uplifted within days of following the bridging practices in the book. Her early years were tough. Growing up the last of eight kids in the Depression, starting at age ten she had to clean homes to help with the family's finances; her mother, bedridden with rheumatoid arthritis, was unloving and distant. As a mother, Jeanette had been difficult, trying to control her children's and grandchildren's lives, living vicariously through them, giving unwelcome advice, and openly criticizing them. Her relationship with her family was, understandably, tenuous. After unsuccessful traditional psychotherapies in her sixties, she came to one of my workshops and began a bridging practice. Within a week of her first session, she was able to see that what happened in her childhood had not permanently damaged her. What was damaging her were her thoughts, returning to the memory over and over again. As Jeanette saw that this was how her Identity System was seeking to control her and limit her to a damaged self, she became more relaxed and more outgoing, stopped criticizing, and starting listening to her children. To her great surprise, her family began reaching out to her. She began studying art. A neighbor noted her personality change and asked Jeanette if she was on Prozac! Another neighbor said, "Gee whiz, how'd you get rid of that chip on your shoulder? I've known you for twenty years. How did it happen?"

In my workshops, people frequently want to know how healing and transformation can be so simple. They wonder how the techniques in this book—listening to background sounds, tuning in to body sensations, and sensing what they touch—can transform their lives. Their Identity System won't let them trust in their own innate ability to heal themselves. But for them, and for you, to find that limitless healing and the sense of your own possibilities, all you have to do is come to your senses.

That said, I have found that while most people understand what the words mean, modern life has so separated us from our senses that we need some guidance to show us the way. And that is what this book is about. In it, you'll find an elegantly simple and powerful way to live a more natural, joyful life. Within hours, you can begin a life-changing transformation. Whether you want to be a better parent, friend, or partner; improve your performance at work or in competition; lose weight; or end an unhealthy addiction, *Come to Your Senses* will help you change in profound yet basic ways. Chronic pain sufferers will experience the true healing power of their body, and those who struggle with anger, depression, or anxiety will find that their perspective—and their lives—are altered when they let their own body's inner wisdom guide them and stop listening to their old, self-destructive self-talk. Whatever you desire from your life, when you come to your senses, you'll come to a peace and a clarity that will guide you through whatever life brings you.

In the chapters that follow, I've incorporated exercises and experiences from workshops and private consultations covering nearly four decades. The skills described in *Come to Your Senses* have been refined over many years of practical application. I am certain they will bring healing and harmony into your life. Use them to explore your own personal wisdom and the powers of self-healing that are your birthright.

1

Healing Begins with Your Identity System

From an early age, we are taught how to take care of our bodies. We learn to wash our hair, brush our teeth, and clip our nails. We are told to exercise our muscles, and we are cautioned against eating unhealthy foods. We learn what our parents and teachers feel is important for living happy, productive lives.

Yet we rarely, if ever, are taught what to do with our thoughts. Of course, some thoughts we don't need to *do* anything about; they come and go as harmlessly as birds flying in and out of our field of vision. But too many others stick in our heads like flies to flypaper. Some stay for years, even a lifetime, creating a head full of worry, clutter, and noise—a sticky state of being that adversely affects every aspect of life. What creates this glue that holds our thoughts in our minds long after they've outlived their usefulness? This glue is manufactured by our Identity System, a system not unlike the other systems that keep our bodies ticking: the central nervous system, cardiovascular system, gastrointestinal system, and so on.

The human Identity System evolved in order to confirm and deepen the separateness of family, clan, religion, culture, race, nation, and species—i.e., to help us create our individual identity. Thus by definition, the Identity System is composed of self-centered thoughts. Without it, humans would lack self-interest, direction, and drive. However, though its purpose is to provide for human individuation and social structure by which we can survive, the Identity System does limit human development through separation. This need for separation has mixed evolutionary consequences: individuals and civilizations have matured and flourished through the development of their Identity Systems. Steven Pinker, in his book *The Blank Slate*, makes a strong case for a genetic component to the Identity System. He writes that common to all societies are such inventions as personal names, taboos, marriage, government, tools, and economic inequalities. Other common innate traits of individuation are aggression, violence, weapons, sexual jealousy, envy, and modesty.

In itself, the Identity System is not the problem. The problem comes when it becomes dominant, preventing the ideal interplay between separation (the Identity System) and union (the Source). The Identity System is helpful only up to the point where development of your self becomes rigid and exclusive—when your Identity System story is all that you are, all that you can be, and when you do not know how to rest it. Whenever it is overactive, it restricts awareness, creates fear, and disrupts the harmony and balance of the mind-body connection. This false and limited vision impairs not only how you experience yourself but your activities as well, reducing you to being only as good as your last thought. But this is of course a fallacy. All thoughts are merely the result of a brain cell secreting a neurotransmitter. Getting to know your Identity System and its operations is essential to freeing you from self-limiting thoughts.

The Identity System is not the ego, the "CEO" of our psyche, which Sigmund Freud described as that part of the mind which experiences and reacts to the world, mediating between inner needs and the demands of society. As such, the ego can be characterized by natural functions such as hearing, seeing, remembering, thinking, relating to others, feeling, and acting. The Identity System's exaggerated self-interest, in contrast, creates an identity that lacks authenticity—because it is not complete—and interferes with the natural functioning in your everyday life.

Identity System Requirements

Your Identity System is based on specific thoughts that I call *requirements*. I have expanded upon the work of Charlotte Joko Beck, who in her thirty years of teaching and her two books, *Nothing Special* and *Everyday Zen*, has used the concept of *requirements* as well as many of the awareness practices mentioned in later chapters. These requirements reinforce the damaged self (a dysfunctional state of the body-mind) and dictate how you should be and how the world should be at each moment. Whenever you feel that these requirements are unfulfilled, you experience the symptoms of an activated Identity System—tension, fear, and physical distress. Because they are manifestations of the damaged self, your Identity System requirements cause you to fruitlessly expend energy trying to satisfy them. Here's a brief example of requirements and how they bring a person down:

Isabella, a sales clerk in a boutique, would go home irritated, exhausted, and resentful after listening to a day's worth of gossip from her co-workers and the demands of her customers. After several weeks of following the techniques described in this book, she noticed an effortless change in the way she viewed her work. When co-workers gossiped, she would smile to herself, aware now that she had the requirement that people shouldn't gossip.

She no longer allowed their actions to dictate her reactions, and instead she focused her attention on her work. When customers were demanding and irritable, she recognized that she had had an unrealistic expectation that she would be able to make every customer happy. Once she recognized this thought, she was able to let it go. Free from that thought, she simply did her best. Now she was able to handle situations that before made her tense and miserable. Her home life improved too—because she was relaxed at work, her evenings with her husband were more light-hearted and easy.

As humans, we share many Identity System requirements, such as "I should do things right," "Life should be better," "I should have more self-control," or "Others should be honest and considerate." When I'm driving and I hit a number of red lights, I start thinking, "Gee, why are there so many red lights? Why don't they have the lights synchronized?" I feel the tension in my chest, and I then look to the requirement that's causing my physical distress: *Stan deserves green lights*. Whenever I don't have green lights, I'm damaged—my body is tense, my mind is cluttered with angry thoughts, and I'm less attentive to the task at hand: driving. Now when I encounter a red light, my awareness of my requirement lets me smile at myself about how red lights can cause my mind-body connection to be damaged. My Identity System rests and functions normally.

Your Identity System takes the natural trials and tribulations of daily life and creates a tension-filled, polarized world of opposites. To this world, it assigns relative values: tall/short, good/bad, success/failure, love/hate. This duality sets up requirements: "I need to strive to be good and to be successful." The opposite of this statement is simply not acceptable to you. This duality also creates a picture of how the world should be: "It shouldn't rain" or "Friends should be honest and faithful." Realize that your true self is so vast that it embraces not only being optimistic, strong, and independent but also their opposites—being pessimistic, weak, and dependent.

The Fallacy of the Damaged Self

When you have a concept of who you are and believe that this is *all* you are, you experience an incomplete self, a limited construct of feelings, sensations, thoughts, and figments of imagination. The true you is wondrously expansive, complete, and inseparable from the Source and all existence. It is fully present each moment, not separate from the chair you sit upon, or the floor, or the earth, or the air you breathe, or your parents, or the food you eat, or the day your parents first met, or the origin of the human race. Your true self is beyond the Identity System's conceptions of being separate or connected. Everything is connected and interdependent, and yet each of us is unique and separate at each moment. Our dualistic mind has difficulty trying to conceptualize this paradox, which can be illustrated by an electron: when observed as a particle, it behaves like a particle and has boundaries. When observed as a wave, it behaves like a wave and possesses moving boundaries. Its essence responds to the observer's point of view. Our own limitless connection to the Source and all energy is shown by Nima Arkani Hamed, a theoretical particle physicist at the University of California at Berkeley, when he once asked, "How much of the universe can you pinch between your thumb and your forefinger?"

He answers his own question: "Maybe a lot more than you think. Far reaches of the cosmos may be less than a millimeter away. Whole other universes may be within your grasp. Even if you cannot see these distant places and other worlds, you may be in communication with them through the most familiar forces, gravity."

A limited, damaged version of yourself can affect your entire life, as my dialogue with Julie shows:

Julie: "You keep saying I'm not really damaged, but I can't believe that."

Stan: "It's the Identity System that continually reinforces the idea that you're damaged."

Julie: "No! My father abused me. I can't see what that has to do with my Identity System."

Stan: "Yes, you suffered severe trauma. But just take a moment right now, close your eyes, and search inside to find where you are damaged." (Julie does this, and after a few moments the following exchange takes place.)

Stan: "Julie, did you find any damage?"

Julie: "It's that my father abused me."

Stan: "But that is a thought. 'My father abused me' is just a thought. Where is the damage?"

Julie: "I don't understand. What he did to me created this damage that has made my life miserable, and I try to live with those painful memories."

Stan: "What he did was horrible and wrong. But Julie, today, right here in this room, the damage inflicted upon you is only captured thoughts from the Identity System. These thoughts are, 'I was abused by my father, so I am damaged,' or 'Since I was abused by my father, I must be damaged.' Still, these are only thoughts."

Julie: "But what about the psychological damage? I carry scars of my early trauma. I see that as damaged."

Stan: "When you cut your finger, your body naturally responds and the wound heals. You might have a scar, but the scar is not the damage itself—merely a visual sign of a healed wound. If the wound doesn't heal for some reason, that is a sign that your natural healing function is impaired. Psychological trauma is no different from physical trauma. When a psychological trauma occurs, even something horrific, we have a natural ability to heal. When, however, the psychological wound doesn't heal, again that is a sign that your natural healing function is impaired. And what impairs it is your Identity System, which, by capturing your thoughts, is creating and re-creating your sense of damage."

Julie: "So what you're saying is that my father didn't really damage me; he hurt me, but it's my Identity System that has made it seem like permanent damage?"

Stan: "Yes, the Identity System's mission is to continually reinforce your damaged self and to cajole you into believing that you are only that damage. Look inside again and see if you can find any damage. Close your eyes and slowly and carefully explore your mind for the damage. Look far to the right, then to the left, up, down, backward, and forward. See if you can find any damage."

Julie: "I couldn't find any damage—just space. But there were thoughts about me being victimized."

Stan: "Yes, these thoughts naturally arise in the pure space of the mind. The key is to recognize when your Identity System is activating the damage and preventing you from experiencing the spaciousness, functioning, and healing of your Source-fed true self. Who you are—your true self—is so vast and boundless that you can't be damaged. Thoughts are just thoughts."

Once she began to recognize her own Identity System, Julie was able to move beyond her limited identity as a victim and begin to transform her life, living with joy and an expanded sense of who she really is.

Since my discovery of the Identity System, I have found that all of us, even those who have not experienced traumas like

Julie's, have a damaged self due to an overactive Identity System. Once activated, the Identity System gains control of our mind-body connection, and we come to experience ourselves as impaired in value and functioning. I have used the practices in this book to work with thousands of people like Julie who want to live life more fully.

Your Personal Storylines

Your Identity System allows the damaged self to thrive via storylines or daily dramas you construct. "My life should have meaning; I need to make a difference" is a requirement whose related storyline might go something like this: "I'm just not doing anything important; why don't I shape up; what am I missing?" When your Identity System is in control, you're immersed in a complete story about the past or the future that takes you away from the here and now, contracts your awareness, clutters your mind, and makes you physically tense. The more you tune in to the reruns on "Channel Me," the more you cover up the mental, physical, and spiritual aspects of who you really are. When the Identity System rests, i.e., when you recognize your requirements and storylines and can move easily past them, your true and fully functioning self can thrive. The most important thing to remember here is that the damaged self is a 100 percent false belief—you are not really damaged. You are whole and magnificently complete. Awareness will dissolve your storylines and allow your natural self to manifest. Here are examples from my workshops:

Ron grew up in a lower-class area of Detroit. Although he is now living in an affluent San Francisco suburb and is a successful and gregarious professional and civic leader, he always felt that he needed to be "twice as good as the next guy." He never discussed this sense of inferiority with anyone, considering it a normal carryover from his childhood. When Ron learned about storylines, he clearly saw how frequently his own storyline about having to prove himself over and over played in his mind, leading to his familiar feeling of never being good enough and the tension that accompanied it. From that moment on, Ron envisioned his storylines to be "foreign bodies" that demanded his attention. As he began to intercept them earlier and earlier, to his amazement he came to a new peace of mind and sense of well-being.

His wife, Liz, saw the difference in Ron, and she came to the next series of workshops. She is an attractive executive in the cosmetics industry with a trim figure and impeccable grooming. Behind the façade, however, Liz was suffering from an eating disorder. Prior attempts at analyzing the basis of her problem in psychotherapy did not persuade her that she was anything but fat, unattractive, and unlovable. After we discussed storylines, Liz remarked, "My thoughts are true; they are not fantasy storylines. Look at my stubby fingers. You should see my thighs and all the blemishes under my makeup."

I responded, "The main point is not whether the stories are true or false but how often you play them throughout your day. I would like you to observe whenever these storylines come up. Whenever you note them, momentarily become aware of the sounds in the background, sense what your hands are touching and doing, and then return to whatever you are doing at the moment."

In the next class, Liz commented, "I'm amazed how invasive these storylines are. They go on all day. As soon as I become aware of them and get back to my job, I become more relaxed."

By becoming aware, Liz was finally able to move past her old storyline, and her life changed. As she recognized that her storylines were holding her damaged self together and driving her eating disorder, her weight and physical shortcomings slowly became non-issues. Her concept of herself had expanded beyond her obsession over her appearance.

Your Identity System Doesn't Want You to Change

It's sometimes easier for us to limit our perceptions than to be aware of the myriad of options and situations that could face us. Your Identity System helps you limit yourself by giving you a fixed and separate identity. The price, however, is anxiety, excess worry, body tension, and restricted awareness. In short, it limits you from experiencing and expressing the vast and rich vitality of who you really are. Bruce Lee seemed to sum up the damaged self of the Identity System when he wrote, "Because one does not want to be disturbed, to be made uncertain, he establishes a pattern of conduct, of thought, a pattern of relationships. He then becomes a slave to the pattern and takes the pattern to be the real thing." The real thing he refers to is not the damaged self the Identity System constructs for you but rather a life of natural functioning unconstrained by self-limiting storylines.

To help understand the Identity System's effects on us and why we would want to rest it, I sometimes ask participants in my workshops to imagine what the Identity System's effect would be on an eagle. Some people say that it puts the eagle in a cage so he can't fly where he chooses or feel the wind or observe the vistas ahead of him. Others say the Identity System is a tether that doesn't allow the eagle to experience the heights of its possibilities. The best analogy I've heard is from a young man who said that the Identity System doesn't prevent the eagle from flying. It prevents the eagle from appreciating the vastness of who he is and what he's doing. He doesn't experience his seeing and soaring in the marrow of his bones. He doesn't appreciate the enormous overview he has of the world. The Identity System numbs him out. The young man said, "It would be just like if I took a shower in a raincoat. That's what the Identity System does to me—it numbs me. So I am living my life, flying through my life, but I don't experience the wholeness of my true self because my Identity System has disembodied me, closing down my senses, closing down who I really am."

The Identity System takes you away from the present moment, as noted by these comments from my workshops:

Brett: "Often when I'm driving along the freeway I get completely lost in my thoughts. Five miles of beautiful scenery go by and I don't even notice it. Later I even miss my exit. I guess that's also dangerous—I might miss another driver's signal or cause an accident."

Debra: "I get so tense at board meetings that five minutes will go by and I'll not have heard a word, and then someone will ask my opinion and I need to fabricate a response. It's as if I try to pull myself up by my bootstraps. I try to appear calm but my insides are really upset."

Sylvia: "My boyfriend will call and we'll talk, but within seconds I'm not hearing anything. I feel so zoned out and nervous and he can sense it. He gets angry and I don't know what to say. I don't know why I space out like that."

Juan: "I'll be having sex with my wife and then find myself thinking about work and what I had for dinner, and then I'll start berating myself for thinking about such things, and then suddenly I feel horrible and angry at myself."

Tom: "I'm on the golf course, preoccupied by work and finances. I try to relax but of course end up slicing the ball."

Lost in our daily dramas, we even become insensitive to our own bodies! Yet this doesn't make the Identity System the enemy. On the contrary, it is a blessing, because not only does it show you a road map of what is causing your dissatisfaction and suffering, but it also points the way to your natural self.

Bridging Awareness

The purpose of this book is to give you a new and exciting way of looking at your life and to provide you with tools to "rest" your overactive Identity System. When you shift your awareness to a sight, a sound, or a sensation of your body, you put the engine of your Identity System on idle. When I started working with people to develop the necessary tools to rest the Identity System, I called the tools and the balanced physical, mental, and spiritual state they facilitate *bridging*. Bridging allows your natural functioning (i.e., living freely, with a resting Identity System) to flow. Bridging is living your life at its best—natural living. Bridging reaches every cell, every atom in your body, right to the essence of your being, transforming how you enjoy nature, relate to family and friends, play golf or tennis, have sex, make money, pray, care for yourself and others, or be more successful at work. Bridging transforms your immune system and creates balance and harmony in your biological systems. It connects you to your Source.

If all these facets of your life are not transformed, you are not bridging, because bridging is not *separate* from the normal activities of daily living. It *is* living—freely and fully. You don't need to interrupt your life to bridge.

Bridging practice has two wings. The first is the awareness practice that allows the Identity System to rest. With awareness you come back to the present moment and are cognizant of the sights, sounds, physical sensations, and thoughts washing over you, whether you are tense or relaxed, happy or miserable, clear or confused.

The second wing of bridging is befriending your Identity System, which means recognizing and being familiar with its requirements and how they restrict your life. You do this through mind-body mapping, which you'll learn more about in chapter 5. Awareness of your Identity System is all it takes to rest it.

Bridging is a natural part of all of us. It is simply using the body's wisdom to live our life at its best. As adults, we forget our innate ability to expand our consciousness beyond our worries and pains. After I encouraged a skeptic in one of my pain seminars to bridge by tuning in to background sounds, he acknowledged afterwards that it was a technique he had used long ago: "I remember when I was a young boy and I had a lot of pain, I'd go lie down by the river; when I closed my eyes and listened to it talk, the pain would just sort of drift off."

With a resting Identity System, we function naturally. Each body system, each organ, each cell does its work, and we take actions that are appropriate to circumstances. For example, a natural response to fatigue is that we get into bed and sleep. However, if our mind is cluttered with thoughts and our body is tense, our Identity System interferes with the natural function of sleep. Imagine a baseball pitcher when his Identity System takes over: "I gave up a home run; I'm not doing well now; I'm losing my stuff. Have to try harder." He is so wrapped up in his thoughts at this point that the natural function of throwing a baseball is impaired.

This natural functioning manifests our true, or natural, self—a self that cannot be grasped by our thinking mind, and a self that can come to life only when we rest our Identity System. The natural self always manifests when the Identity System rests. In this book, you'll learn how to give a rest to your Identity System and its assistants: the "depressor," with its motto, "I'm not good enough"; and the "fixer," with its motto, "Always try harder." Both the depressor and the fixer fuel the damaged self, thereby creating imbalance in the mind-body connection.

How do you recognize your own Identity System? It's actually quite simple. Take a minute now to do a quick experiment that will get you started on the most important transformation of your life. Wherever you are—in your house, outdoors, on a train, or elsewhere—shift your attention from reading this book to listening to any nonverbal sound. It could be the hum of the fluorescent lighting, birds' chirping, or the traffic's roar. Music and voices do not work. Focus on the sound and notice what happens to it when you have a thought.

You'll quickly notice two things. First, when you initially shift your attention to the sound, the thoughts in your head take a backseat to the act of hearing; your awareness expands and your body relaxes. Second, soon after you shift your attention to the sound, you'll notice your thoughts trying once again to take center stage: "I've got bills to pay," "This exercise is stupid," and so on. When a thought arises and you are wrapped up in its drama, your awareness then narrows. You no longer hear the sound; your body tenses. This is your Identity System at work.

Demystifying the Mind-Body Connection

The diagram that follows unlocks the mystery of the mind-body connection and shows schematically the difference between natural functioning and an Identity System–driven life. Both loops begin with a thought. The Natural Loop shows how thoughts, remaining free of any interference, generate natural functioning and a unified mind-body connection. In the Identity System Loop, the same thought is entrapped by the depressor/fixer cycle and impairs functioning and disrupts the mind-body connection. This physical/mental state is the damaged self. Awareness, through bridging, interrupts the Identity System Loop, creates free thoughts, and normalizes your mind-body connection. Then your body's wisdom transforms your life.

With a Resting Identity System, All Problems Have Solutions

You, me, the person living in the house next door—all of us have had some form of trauma in our lives, traumas that range in form

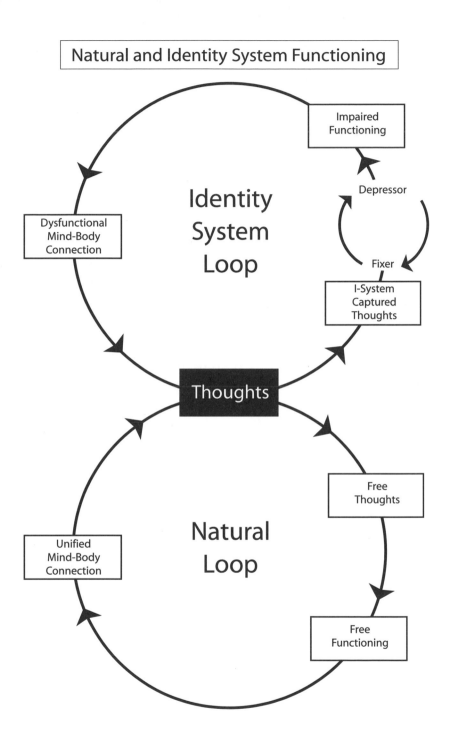

and hue from the horrific, such as the violence of war, to the commonplace, such as suffering rejection from a close friend. If you take nothing else from this book, remember this: No matter what traumas you have been through, it is your Identity System—not the events themselves—that keeps you from experiencing life at its best.

Without a doubt, life can be painful. But the joy is that you and I are much more than the sum total of our past and present problems. It is these problems that the Identity System is so good at cataloging and reminding us of. Will Rogers once said, "If you find yourself in a hole, the first thing you do is stop digging." The existence of the Identity System depends on continued digging. It is our task to stop digging ourselves into holes and to rest our Identity System so we can put our problems in their proper perspective.

To demonstrate the power of the Identity System to perpetuate problems, I ask new workshop participants to jot down three major problems present in their lives. Here are some typical problems people have listed:

"My husband doesn't love me as much as he used to."

"She is always complaining."

"I can't enjoy life because of my back pain."

"I eat too much."

"I can't stop drinking."

"My life is miserable."

"I'm depressed."

"I'm always sick."

"People always disappoint me."

"My daughter might get pregnant."

"I wilt when the going gets tough."

"I don't have enough money."

Carla, one of my workshop attendees, is in her early thirties and is bright and verbal with an easygoing manner. Her most frustrating problem is that her boss doesn't appreciate her. Carla's problem map follows. Mind-body mapping (which I'll explain in later chapters) is one of the most important things you can do to recognize and rest your Identity System. By creating a map such as this you can pinpoint your Identity System's machinations, allowing you to recognize them when they appear again. At the center of Carla's map is her problem: "My boss doesn't appreciate me." Initially when she finished the map, she grimaced and said that seeing it made her feel even angrier at her boss and that her whole life was tangled up in this anger.

Carla's map is overflowing with "boss stuff." It seems to take for granted that a mind state filled with boss stuff is a natural and inevitable result of her boss's behavior. But is it? The real problem is not the boss's behavior but how Carla's Identity System uses that behavior to clutter Carla's mind, create body tension, and impair her functioning. Her map shows how her storylines help Carla experience herself as damaged: "My whole body gets tense when I think how she treats me," "She takes me for granted," and "Why doesn't she like me?"

With a cluttered mind and a body full of tension, we, like Carla, can *only* experience our self as incomplete and damaged. It is precisely this deep-rooted inner sense of damage that Carla's Identity System tries to fix with other thoughts on the map, such as "I'm great; she's the problem," and "If only Robert was my boss—he appreciates me." It's the great "If only...."

The thoughts are not Carla's problem. Every item on Carla's map originates from a completely free and perfectly natural

Carla's Problem Map

She takes me for granted.

I can't afford to quit.

I'm so mad at her.

Why doesn't she like me?

I'll look for another job, and she'll be sorry.

My Boss Doesn't Appreciate Me.

I'm worth 30 percent more money.

If only Robert was my boss—he appreciates me.

I'm great; she's the problem.

Where would she be without me?

She promises me less work but she still piles it on every day.

My whole body gets tense when I think how she treats me.

thought. There is nothing inherently wrong with "I'm great; she's the problem," or "I'll look for another job." The problem is that Carla's Identity System grabs onto these thoughts and uses them to reinforce her own perspective on having a damaged self. That said, Carla still has a hard time understanding that it is her Identity System and not her boss's behavior that is the cause of her problem. We had this discussion:

Carla: "I'm willing to see all sides of this and to look into the evidence my map presents. At the same time, my boss *is* a problem and *has* a problem, and this affects my life."

Stan: "There is no denying that. We are looking now at the possibility that your Identity System has converted a natural life problem—which your natural functioning could solve—into a problem driven by your damaged self, which *cannot* be solved. Mapping shows you how your Identity System has trapped you. It helps you figure out the difference between natural thoughts and Identity System thoughts."

Carla: "I think it's perfectly natural to want people to like me and to seek to improve my life."

Stan: "Those are perfectly natural thoughts. Your Identity System has the *requirement* that your boss should appreciate you. When that requirement isn't met, you feel damaged. Yet the kicker is the fact that your Identity System will never be appeased no matter how much your boss appreciates you. Its mission is to reinforce your damage and incompleteness."

Carla: "That's what you mean when you say that Identity System problems cannot be solved but natural problems can be?"

Stan: "That's correct. As we move through the exercises, we will gain more and more experience and expertise at

recognizing when our Identity System is functioning—and believe me, that's more than half the battle."

David's is another example of a problem map. He has a different storyline than Carla. Instead of trying to heal or fix the damaged self by changes in the outer world, as Carla's map proposes,
David's map points the sharp edge toward himself, but not with a
ready, relaxed mind. Despite the fact that he is successful in his
work and has a caring wife, David's map is full of self-criticism:
"I should be better," "I don't eat right," "I cause my headaches
because I can't sleep," and "I am not organized enough." These
thoughts also originated as helpful, free thoughts. It's completely
natural to think that you need to get up earlier, be more organized, and be more relaxed. However, David's Identity System
grabs these thoughts, using them to clutter his mind and fill his
body with tension.

David's awareness is limited because he is so focused on himself as the problem. This self-condemnation is what is sustaining
the damaged self. No matter how hard David tries, he cannot
resolve his Identity System–driven problems. David's efforts to fix
himself are fueled by the damaged self and serve only to reinforce
the damage. He is unable to manifest the natural free functioning
that is needed for problem solving.

The Problem Map

Take time now to complete your first problem map. It will help
you get a sense of your own Identity System patterns and flash
points. As you move through this book, you'll be working on
many maps—as well as bridging exercises. Hold on to these problem maps; you'll be referring to them again in the next chapter.

Start by looking at your life. What are your three biggest problems? Write each one of them out in a sentence. Now close your
eyes and envision your life if your problems were resolved. Next,

David's Problem Map

I got up too late again today.

I am not organized enough.

My stomach is tight.

It takes so long to get to sleep.

I cause my headaches because I can't sleep.

I Need More Self-Control.

I try to relax, but I'm scared I'll mess up.

I am not satisfied with the way I am.

I should be exercising regularly, but I don't.

I should be better.

I don't eat right.

write down your most difficult problem in the middle of a blank piece of paper. Draw a circle around the sentence, and think about the problem by letting thoughts arise naturally. Take no more than five minutes to jot down what comes up in your mind regarding the problem, writing each thought in a few words anywhere on the paper. Let your thoughts bubble up randomly, and include any physical sensations. Break the continuity of your thinking by scattering the thoughts about on the paper. Don't analyze or elaborate upon the thoughts or correct the words.

When you're done, observe your *current* emotional reaction to your problem statement. Then review each item on your map and note your body's reaction to it as well as any additional thoughts. Reactions of frustration, worry, anger, disappointment, fear, anxiety, guilt, shame, blaming, self-condemnation, and especially body tension point to the Identity System's involvement. Just remember that this map is not your life but is merely a snapshot of your Identity System in action.

The problem map has been enormously successful in pinpointing for individuals the root of their unease. For many, the effect is of a revelation that opens the door to a whole new existence, as the following example shows:

Fred and his wife, Kathy, owned a small, well-established software company. In a two-hour session, employees of the company mapped their biggest problem. Fred shared his map with the group; his problem was "not having enough money to launch a new product." Risktaking and financial items were listed, but the predominant theme of the map was Fred's self-doubt and self-criticism. Physically, he manifested his tension by hunching over and becoming tearful as he expressed how badly he felt about this problem. As he talked, however, he suddenly brightened and exclaimed, "Look what I'm doing to myself! It's not our finances that are causing my distress—it's my Identity System." His revelation continued later in the day as he was giving me a tour of the company. We entered Kathy's office where she, a gifted multi-tasker, was working at her computer even as Fred began talking to her. He interrupted himself to say with wonder, "I have a requirement that Kathy should stop what she's doing when I talk to her. Before, I have gotten tense and angry, burning up inside with thoughts of rejection. Now, it's different. I see that it's just my requirement, and Kathy is free to be however she wants to be. It doesn't seem like a problem anymore!"

These life-transforming experiences are not transient but are the long-lasting natural effects of bridging. As long as you continue using the tools in this book, you will be able to make this same instantaneous and progressive change for the better. David, Carla, Fred, and now you have taken the first step in resting your Identity System, which is to map its activities. Once your Identity System is exposed to the light of day and to your growing awareness, you can move beyond self-limiting thoughts to the expansiveness that is your birthright as a human being.

2

Recognize Your Own Identity System and How It Works

Life has its vicissitudes. Most of us attribute the downs to outside stresses—job issues, financial demands, family pressures, insufficient time—or to our perceived internal deficiencies. When we are down, we feel burned out. The daily grind is too much. Our body is full of aches and feels tired and heavy. Breathing is shallow, our shoulders are hunched, our head is tight. Our mind is full of worries and irritation. We vacillate from self-deprecation to resignation to blaming others. We try harder, work harder, but to no avail.

Others may not notice the downs, but they weigh on us. No matter what we accomplish, we have little sense of fulfillment or peace of mind. We are driven and can't relax. We try for the gold ring, and with grit and determination, we obtain it. But the prize is empty. We have made millions but don't feel like a million. Our bodies are racing. Our minds are cluttered. Our hearts are empty. Our souls are isolated.

These conditions are not a natural part of life. They are not due to genetics, upbringing, trauma, environmental stresses, or even personality. These conditions are associated with the damaged self and are the result of the Identity System's two helpers, the depressor and the fixer. The depressor captures your free thoughts to reinforce a sense of damage. It is the direct verbalization of the damaged self. The fixer captures free thoughts in attempts to fix the damage. Because the damage it seeks to fix is illusory, the fixer's work is never complete. Although the depressor and the fixer are readily apparent, if you don't know what you are looking for, you will never find them.

By learning to recognize your own depressor and fixer requirements, you can rest your Identity System and live your life at its best.

Meet Your Depressor

Your mind works with a full range of thoughts. Just as day cannot exist without night, your mind can't conceive a thought without conceiving its opposite. Natural mind functioning includes both positive and negative thoughts; you can never rid yourself of them. In fact, trying to get rid of them only gives them more energy.

What are you to do, for example, when you think, "I'll never get this right," "I'm lazy," "I'm not good enough," "I don't have enough self-control," or "I'm not clever enough"? These appear to be negative thoughts you should avoid. On the contrary, they are wonderful, natural thoughts. The problem arises when the depressor steps in and creates a body-mind that is full of misery. Let's look at an example. The thought "My husband forgot our anniversary" leads to a storyline like "He doesn't appreciate me; why did he forget? What did I do? Am I lovable? Mother said no one would ever love me. I have been jilted before...."

The depressor takes an innocent thought and runs with it, cluttering the person's mind with a storyline and adversely impacting the body with fear and tension. The collapsing awareness, fear, and tension lead to an experience of damage. The person is no longer having just a thought but a total body experience. We have all experienced this train of runaway thoughts. Our own Identity System takes a wound and, rather than letting it heal, pours salt into it. A simple medical model of the brain's bipolar sites shows how the Identity System works. One site, the mania site, speeds up mental and physical processes. (When this site is pathologically overstimulated, it leads to a manic type of bipolar disorder.) The depressive site slows us down. Our body naturally functions to keep both sites in balance. The Identity System's depressor is so powerful because the thoughts it captures trigger activities of the depressive brain site and alters every cell and organ system in our body. The harmless thought "I'm worthless" leads to contraction of our entire metabolism. The depressor has converted a naturally functioning mind-body connection into a dysfunctional mind-body connection.

Meet Your Fixer

"I'm weak and helpless and must find someone perfect to take care of me." This is an example of a fixer requirement, a thought designed to repair the damaged self. The "I'm weak and helpless" part is often repressed and masked over for a more positive appearance. The fixer uses the brain's mania site, creating motivation and pressure. Finding that "perfect person" becomes more important than taking care of one's own self. However, no person, no matter how perfect, can heal your damaged self, and the drive to find that person results in only more misery.

The Identity System functions equally well with either positive-sounding requirements such as "I want to be a good, kind, and compassionate person" or negative-sounding requirements such as "I want to have my way, no matter what." In one of my workshops for clergy members, a pastor said that as he counsels people, he tries to remedy their problems—which is a positive goal. After understanding the role of the Identity System, he said,

"I think that the source of my advice is often my fixer, and not my natural self." Many non-clergy counselors and therapists come to the same realization that much of their work has been to support the client's or patient's Identity System, which ultimately perpetuates the person's limited self. With bridging, they allow others to use their own free-functioning selves to solve their problems and are able to facilitate transformations that years of treatment had not accomplished.

Natural thoughts are easily transformed by the Identity System into requirements. Telling one from the other is key. The difference is that "I'm damaged" is hidden somewhere within an Identity System requirement, such as "I must take care of myself," "I need to be in control," "I must eat right and exercise daily," or "I shouldn't get sick." Let's take the requirement "I shouldn't get sick." What happens when you do get sick? Your Identity System will cause you to be angry with yourself. You will be inhibited by worry and resentfulness because being sick will confirm your notion of damage and limitation. Remember that "I shouldn't get sick" is a natural and appropriate thought about staying well. With a resting Identity System, you will simply be free to heal and take care of yourself. Your body will not fill with tension and your mind will not fill with self-condemnation if you do fall ill. Natural thoughts foster healing, while requirements create mental and physical disease.

Roger, a middle-aged physician, was struggling with the distinction between natural thoughts and Identity System requirements and between natural functioning and Identity System–driven functioning. The next time we met, however, he said he was now able to clearly see the difference.

Roger reported, "I went to the gym after work, acting on the thought that I needed exercise. The thought and action 'Go to the gym' were natural, without pressure. I was relaxed and paying attention to my body doing leg presses. Again, natural function. I looked around and saw a couple of young guys pressing humongous stacks of weights. My Identity System took over: 'I'm not so puny. I can press more weights than I'm doing. What if they look over here and see my dinky stack of weights?'

"I immediately added forty pounds more. 'I'll show them what the doctor can do.' As I pressed this load of weights, my back started to hurt. It's still a bit tender now, but seeing my depressor and fixer get the best of me was a great revelation. I'm starting to note my bodily sensations like jaw tension and tightening in my chest when my fixer is in action, like when I'm home with the kids. Once I recognize it, my body relaxes and I have choices. Being a father is easier now. I'm not damaged if they are mad at me."

The Identity System generates distrust of your self and the world. Your fixer requirements drive you to establish how you and the world should be. When these requirements are fulfilled, the depressor says it's not good enough or you become fearful the good situation won't last. When your requirements aren't fulfilled, fear and anxiety—the Identity System's backbone—create physical tension and restrict your awareness to a point where a crisis arises. In addition, when the fixer's repairs don't work, the depressor jumps back into action again. When you create your fixer map in chapter 5, you'll see a corresponding depressor underneath each fixer statement.

From David's and Carla's problem maps in the last chapter, examples of the fixer are "I'll look for another job, and she'll be sorry," "I'm great; she's the problem," "I'm worth 30 percent more money," "If only Robert was my boss—he appreciates me," "I am not organized enough," and "I should be exercising regularly, but I don't." On the map you created, can you find examples of the fixer in action?

Unmasking Your Identity System

To get an idea of how tightly your Identity System controls your life, do a one-minute exercise. Sit back, relax, and close your eyes.

Breathe deeply and naturally, and count each exhalation. Each time a thought intervenes, start over. Notice what number you can reach before a thought intervenes. Most people make it to only a few counts. Such is the power of the Identity System. Although this is a simple example, it serves to demonstrate how the Identity System interferes with your free functioning. It does that continuously throughout the day.

Because the Identity System can disguise itself through fixer and depressor requirements, it's important to view it from many different angles. One of its tricks is to polarize our interactions according to self/other orientation. We experience a dualistic world rather than a natural, unified world of harmonious differences. For instance, suppose you are about to meet someone new: perhaps a prospective mother-in-law, your daughter's new boyfriend, or a blind date. As you walk to the door to receive your guest, your Identity System has you wondering what the person looks like, where he or she comes from, and whether or not you will like him or her. Your Identity System piles all this on top of the natural relationship between a host and a guest. You easily become so busy weaving thoughts into your storyline that you are not at ease and naturally welcoming. Your visitor senses that he or she is on trial, and thus a simple situation is fraught with tension. Your Identity System distorts both your behavior and your personality; it has intervened and restricted your awareness of the outside world.

In addition to reviewing your problem maps for Identity System activity, quietly review the past days, weeks, or years. Can you begin to see the role the depressor and fixer have played? Note that when you have accomplished a goal, peace of mind eludes you because your depressor has "picked apart" your success and moved your fixer to set other goals. Bring your awareness to your tension and worries, and observe how the Identity System disrupts your sense of well-being and free functioning, keeping your mind occupied with an endless string of problems. Start to embrace the possibility that the Identity System is driving your problems and preventing you from naturally resolving them.

Once your awareness has expanded to embrace the possibility that your Identity System is overactive, your life opens to major transformations. Awareness—which you have tasted and will continue to learn through the bridging exercises in chapter 3—melts down your Identity System, unmasking your fixer and depressor. Your natural mind-body connection begins to heal your whole being. Your true self begins to emerge. As your journey continues, natural problem solving occurs and your character purifies.

In an old fable, a fellow was searching for something under a street lamp. A neighbor walked by and asked, "Have you lost something?"

The man replied, "I'm looking for my house key."

The neighbor said, "I'll help you. About where did you lose it?"

"Over there," the man answered, pointing to a dark alleyway.

"Then why in the world are you looking here?" the neighbor exclaimed.

"Because the light is better here," the man answered.

To find the key to transform your life, you need to know both what you are looking for and where to look. You now know what your Identity System looks like. You know that it is not situations or conditions in life which cause or perpetuate your damaged self. You need only to shine your light of awareness inwardly and rest your Identity System. The next chapter will give you further tools for doing this.

3

Come to Your Senses

How do you know when your Identity System is active and when it is at rest? The answer is simple yet elusive. When you are present in the moment, your Identity System rests. As soon as you are pulled away from the moment by a thought, your Identity System is active. In this chapter, you'll learn practices that help you return to the present moment, with all its richness and texture, instead of letting you dwell in a head swirling with Identity System–driven thoughts.

As with any practice such as meditation or prayer, you may think it is necessary to concentrate in order to expand your awareness. Not true. You are always in—and can never escape being in—the moment. It is impossible! You needn't stretch to expand your awareness. To be present in the moment, you need only come back to your senses. Being in the moment is simply being aware of the sights and sounds around you, your body's sensations, and your thoughts. It requires neither happiness nor relaxation nor health. All that is required is your awareness.

Chapter 1 introduced the concept of bridging awareness. The awareness practices in this chapter connect, or bridge, your current state of contracted consciousness and impaired functioning—the damaged self—to an expanded state of consciousness and natural functioning—your true self. When you are bridging, you are not going anywhere. You are not escaping your current reality in search of a calmer, saner place. You have it all right here, right now. You can act only in the moment; you can be only in the moment; you can live only in the moment. Bridging allows you to experience and express that truth in your life.

Any practice that rests your Identity System is bridging. By restoring your natural mind-body functioning and tuning in to your Source, bridging is also healing; it reduces fear, mind clutter, tension, and organ dysfunction—all manifestations of the damaged self that can seriously impact our physical health. By expanding your awareness, you allow healing to flow.

Here are a few examples of how bridging brings people into the moment:

Before each at-bat, baseball great Ichiro Suzuki picks up the bat with his right hand, extends his right arm, lifts his left hand, touches his right shoulder, and slowly lifts up the fabric of his uniform. After this, he steps up to the plate. Just a superstitious ritual? Not really. Ichiro is preparing himself by resting his Identity System. When he's gripping his uniform, he's bridging; he experiences the texture of his uniform and its elasticity as he pulls the fabric, and he's also consciously aware of gravity as he senses the weight of the bat on his extended arm. In full awareness of his senses and surroundings, his results are impressive: He has one of the top batting averages in major-league baseball.

Fibromyalgia ruled Stephana's life. At forty-one, she required large doses of pain medications and sleeping pills in order to sleep. They weren't working; she was never able to sleep more than two or three hours during the night. She then saw a therapist who used bridging techniques. In the evenings, Stephana started to tune in to background sounds, and she would light a candle so she would be aware of the fragrance; after she blew out the candle, she would climb into bed, paying attention to the texture of the sheets on her body and noting the slight pressure of the mattress on her heels, her buttocks, and her back. Within one week after beginning to attend to her senses, she was able to sleep through the night. With a consistent bridging and mapping practice, she was off most of her medications within several weeks. In fact, when her family saw her, they exclaimed, "Oh, you must be on a new medication! You're looking so well!" Even her physician couldn't believe the physical improvement after a month of her bridging practice. Instead of feeling consumed by the pain of her disease, Stephana is healing and enjoying her days and nights.

When your Identity System is quiet, you experience a sense of spaciousness, lightness, and calmness. Your mind-body connection is balanced. Your mental and physical activities are harmonized. Because self-centered thoughts are resting and consciousness is expanded, bridging allows you to have a more intimate relationship to God.

I frequently work with men and women in the clergy. Early in a clergy workshop, after I explained the Identity System and bridging, one of the attendees asked, "If a person is bridging all the time and resting his Identity System, would he be like Jesus?"

My answer to this intriguing question is that rather than becoming more Jesus-like, the person becomes more Tom-like, more Mary-like, or more Sam-like. Bridging the Identity System allows the person to use all his unique attributes to actualize his own true self. This may well be the actualization of the living Jesus within. Conversely, when a person's Identity System is active, she becomes increasingly a caricature of who she thinks she is and a frozen manifestation of her Identity System.

Toward the end of a rather intensive workshop, one of the clergymen explained that when he is in the pulpit, he wears one hat, preaching intimacy with God and the importance of manifesting scriptures in daily life. However, when he is a counselor to his parishioners, he wears a totally different hat, focusing on everyday, secular issues. "Since bridging means always being in an intimate relationship with God," he said, "I am going to be able to wear the same hat all day, every day." Resting the Identity System means that he can function freely, in harmony with God and others, manifesting his natural self, rather than having to choose a self dictated by circumstances. For you too, awareness of your Identity System will release the spiritual, divine underpinning of your being.

Claiming Your Natural Spaciousness

I often do work in pain clinics where mapping and bridging practices have helped patients deal with their chronic pain. I begin the workshop by placing three glass beakers on a table. One beaker holds two ounces, one holds twenty ounces, and one holds sixty ounces of fluid. I fill the two-ounce container to the brim with red-colored water. The two-ounce beaker represents the patients in their present state, and the red water is their pain. Like the beaker, they are filled to the brim with pain, and there is no room for anything else. Pain is constantly in their thoughts and is wracking their bodies.

I then take a big red pipe wrench and clamp it on the two-ounce beaker. "This," I say, pointing to the pipe wrench, "is your Identity System. Its mission is to contract your awareness and make you believe you're damaged. In this case, it insists that you are no more than your pain. It keeps your awareness clamped onto this thought: 'I am in pain, and therefore I'm damaged.'"

I next remove the pipe wrench from the two-ounce beaker and pour the contents of this beaker into the twenty-ounce beaker. Just as resting the Identity System expands one's awareness, the twenty-ounce beaker represents the patients' increased sense of spaciousness and possibilities. The red liquid, still representing the pain, now fills only a tenth of the container. The amount of pain has not necessarily decreased, but the patients' experience of it has.

Through the continued practice of bridging, of being in the moment with all the senses, awareness continues to expand. To illustrate that, I then pour the two ounces of liquid from the twenty-ounce beaker into the sixty-ounce container. By resting the Identity System, we can turn the reality of pain on its head, decreasing our need to do battle and even giving our pain the space to be. Our capacity for natural healing is directly related to the empty space in each container.

During a two-weekend pain seminar, a participant returned the second week and exclaimed, "My house is getting bigger!" He had become more active, was able to climb the stairs into the attic for the first time in five years, and was visiting old friends. As he related better to his family, he felt that spiritually too, his living space was expanding.

The spaciousness that comes from bridging is valuable not only in treating pain but also in treating anger-control issues. In the classic model of treating perpetrators of domestic violence, the client is taught to take a "time-out" when he is becoming excited or irritable, going outside or to another room to remove himself from the situation and settle himself down. Done in conjunction with the "time-out," bridging greatly increases its effectiveness. The client not only removes himself from the situation but then grounds himself in the moment by listening to background sounds—for example, traffic, dogs barking, leaves rustling—and by feeling the tension in his body—the tight jaw, the clenched fist, the shallow breathing. With the greater spaciousness created by bridging, the person is able to act appropriately in the situation. One man said that when his wife started calling him names in the past, he would get angry and even physically assaultive. Now when she calls him names and henpecks him, he is able to bridge and even smile. He no longer needs to take time-outs.

As his awareness expands, the person becomes a more spacious container and the violent thoughts come and go more easily. As his Identity System rests, his body relaxes and the anger never gets a chance to build up and accelerate. Try it yourself the next time you get angry. Coming to your senses causes your body to relax, thereby diminishing the power of your angry thoughts. It's not possible to carry out violent activities with an expanded consciousness and a relaxed body. Angry thoughts will not have a leg to stand on.

Say Good-bye to Your Disembodied Self with Bridging Practices

Today you have touched your underwear, socks, shoes, blouses, pants, knives, forks, paper, pens, doorknobs, keys, chairs, soap, and towels. These items are only the tip of the iceberg in terms of your daily sensory inputs. How many of these hundreds of sensations have you been aware of? If you are like most of us, the answer is very few. Why? Because, like everyone, your Identity System has so contracted your awareness that you become disembodied—removed from the vitality of your senses. We humans inhabit our thoughts too much, at the expense of our physical body and its surrounding realities. Once you release your body's "visceral belief" in the damaged self and come back to your senses, common ailments such as backache, intestinal upset, and high blood pressure dissipate.

Try the following exercise. It will open your eyes—and the rest of your senses—to the incredible way the Identity System limits your awareness to your own thoughts. Slowly and gently rub your fingers over the fabric of your clothing. Choose a coarse fabric for maximum textural input. Pay attention to the feel of the fabric as your fingers pass over it, and attend to the sensations in your fingertips. Keep rubbing the fabric, and notice what happens to these sensations when you have thoughts; you no longer feel the fabric. In fact, you are not even aware of what your fingers are doing! Consciously work to hang on to the sensations. As your mind begins to think of other things, acknowledge the thoughts ("Oh, I see I'm thinking that I need to take the car into the shop") and return to the sensation at your fingertips.

This exercise is a stark example of how the Identity System disembodies you; it is a good one to return to whenever you feel unsettled or can't sleep—simply rub your fingers over a nearby fabric. The return to your senses soothes you and quiets your mind. An example that powerfully illustrates the value of tuning in to touch was told to me by a woman, Frances, in a presentation I gave on using awareness of the Identity System to become more effective as a parent. Frances has a son with severe Attention Deficit Hyperactivity Disorder (ADHD). The only way she had found to settle him down when he became agitated and disruptive was to walk her fingers along his body. "I'd been resting his Identity System all along and didn't even know it!" she exclaimed.

Focusing your awareness on touch is a vital bridging practice. In every busy life are many opportunities to do bridging practices. For instance, when you brush your teeth in the morning, feel the bristles scraping against your gums, hear the quiet swoosh sound your brush makes, and taste the sharp toothpaste flavor in your mouth.

When the telephone rings, most of us jump. Usually you rush to answer, your brain races into high gear—"I wonder who this is?" "I hope it's not so and so," or "I've been looking forward to this call"—and your body tenses. The next time the telephone rings, take a deep breath, experience the sounds in the room in addition to the ringing, notice your posture and your body's sensations, and then slowly move to answer the telephone. Telephone awareness is a wonderful bridging practice that reduces tension, settles your mind, and makes your day more productive and enjoyable.

When you shower, don't let thoughts of your upcoming daily drama make you oblivious to the fabulous sensations of water dancing off your body, of your fingers gently massaging the shampoo into your hair, and of the soothing gurgle of water flowing down the drain. Savoring the feelings and sounds lets you come back to a full-body experience of your shower and of everything that follows in your day ahead.

When waiting in line at the grocery, rather than being disgruntled at the slow-moving line you're stuck in and thereby reinforcing the damaged self, listen to the background sounds— the Muzak, the sound of a small child cajoling his mother, the clatter of shopping carts being stacked together, the electronic beep as each item passes the scanner. Feel your body—the tired ache in your legs, the rumble in your stomach, the weight of your coat on your shoulders. Be aware of how your Identity System is trying to take you away from being present in the moment. Instead of wanting to be out of the store, you are now immersed in the present moment with an expanded awareness. You may even find that waiting in line is an incredibly rich experience!

Another helpful bridging practice is to notice your posture and movements and the effect of gravity on your body. In my workshops I ask, "How many of you are aware of gravity?" Once, in a workshop, eight participants raised their hands. Surprised at this unusually high number, I asked them how they came to be aware of a force that most of us ignore. It turned out that all eight had ridden their motorcycles to the group! Aside from when we fall or lift a heavy object, most of us are unaware of gravity because our Identity Systems have numbed us to its presence.

Let's see how you can use gravity as an aid to return to your senses. With eyes closed, lean slightly to the right. Lean farther, slowly, until you can feel yourself pulled down by gravity to the right. Now come back to the center. Next, lean to the left, forward, and backward. Be aware of your feelings as you approach the limit of your movement and as you return to the point where you feel centered and balanced. When you are centered, balanced, and aligned with gravity, you can become relaxed and confident. Your body can move freely in any direction. You feel resilient and ready to face your ever-changing life. When not aligned with gravity, you experience physical tension and unpleasant mental states that impair awareness, make you less resilient, and limit your readiness to respond.

Bridging is very successful in treating people who have been unable to regulate their eating habits. Once you learn bridging awareness practices, you become more aware of your body's cravings and of hunger sensations. Even if you have no food issues, try this awareness practice: Smell the aroma of your food, feel its weight on your fork or in your hand, note its appearance, and savor the texture in each bite. At every meal, sit a few moments, look at the food, and take the first two or three bites very slowly. The slow eating is not the prescription itself; it merely helps you wake up your body so your true self is eating rather than your damaged self. People who try this report that experiencing the crunchiness and warmth of toast, for example, is such a fulfilling experience that they don't need butter, jam, or honey on it. They appreciate the taste of vegetables more. They're able to use less salt on their food as they experience the vividness of each of the components of what they're eating. By consistently coming back to the present moment, people report that they are able to eat less, and they're able to lose weight.

Robin, a thirty-five-year-old nurse and mother of two children, had been fifty pounds overweight most of her adult life.

Despite a thorough knowledge of nutrition, exercise, and metabolism, Robin had never found a successful diet regimen. In her first session with me, she created a problem map—the same map used by David and Carla in chapter 1. On mapping her number-one problem, weight control, her map was filled with both depressor and fixer thoughts. Her depressor told her, "I'm fat and disgusting," "I just can't do it," "I was born to be fat," "I have no self-discipline," and "One hundred diets and nothing works." Her fixer tried to buck her up with thoughts like "I do everything else well; I'll make it!" "If I just keep below 1,400 calories and ride my exercise bike every day, I'll do it," and "I don't give up easily." Bodily sensations on her weight-control map included shoulder tension and a backache.

As the following conversation shows, Robin had difficulties in seeing that her real problem was not a lack of discipline, genetics, or metabolic dysfunction but rather was solely the result of her Identity System.

> *Robin:* "I'm an expert on weight control. It can't only be my Identity System that's keeping me from losing weight."
>
> *Stan:* "All your information is wonderful and helpful; however, the reason you fail to lose weight is solely that your Identity System has interfered with your normal-functioning mind-body connection and has activated the damaged self. You have been eating to feed not your body's normal food requirements but to nourish your damaged self—and its appetite is far greater than your body's true and natural needs. Both the act of overeating and its result—weight gain—feed your damaged self, the self which tells you that you are born to be fat or that you can't do it. Your Identity System's damaged self doesn't want to change, and so when you have initial successes with weight-loss regi-

mens, the fixer pushes you to try harder while the depressor plays its incessant tapes: 'You're fat,' 'You'll never keep this up,' and so on. This way your damaged self thrives, but at the expense of your true, natural-functioning self."

Robin: "Are you saying that all it would take for me to lose weight is to rest my Identity System? Would that quiet my damaged self?"

Stan: "Yes. With a resting Identity System, your body's innate wisdom has room to function. It is the wisdom that tells you to eat when you physically require food—not when you mentally want it or when it is available. Let your Identity System rest, and your body will heal."

A week after this conversation and after practicing the bridging awareness mentioned above, Robin came back to our group session and we had the following conversation about her changed perspective:

Robin: "A big difference a week makes! It's amazing that when I tune in and become aware of the objects I touch during the day and the background sounds at the hospital or at home, I feel a new sense of calmness. I'm never calm! Since I've been out of college, I've felt like my life has been one big hurried to-do list, and now, just by bridging to sounds and sensations, I feel totally different, more like I can meet the day's challenges and then let them pass me by without getting all worked up over them."

Stan: "Congratulations! You've learned that by resting your Identity System through bridging, you can allow your body's natural wisdom to flow. You see that you can't solve your problems with your head alone."

With mind-body mapping, Robin saw how her Identity System affected not just her weight but her moods too. In her "Peace of Mind" map (see chapter 8 for a full discussion of this mapping process), she saw how it had created requirements that her patients should appreciate her, that her supervisors should lighten up on their demands, and that the doctors should be more collegial with the nurses. As she put it, "When I got home, I'd be a wreck." These requirements were directly related to her weight problem. She had felt damaged and would eat to comfort herself. But with mapping her requirements and continuing a bridging practice that let her tune in to her body's wisdom, Robin felt that her life had done a complete 180-degree turn:

"My job hasn't changed one bit, but in a way, it has changed completely. I'm more relaxed at work, I get things done, and my supervisors' pushing doesn't stress me out. When the doctors act lordly, I smile to myself. I've let go of my requirements. When I get home after a day, even if I've been super busy, I don't feel like I've been overwhelmed. I come back to my senses, and my body helps me relax my head. I used to think it was the other way around. And oddly enough, I'm not that eager to eat; I'm enjoying tuning in to my body and my thoughts, and food doesn't hold the same allure it used to."

After three weeks, Robin had lost seven pounds, and she said that bridging helped her focus on her life as she lived it, not on the life she thought she should be living: "Exercise and diet seem to take care of themselves. I've come to recognize my Identity System requirements, the ones which told me that after a hard day I deserve a dessert, that a good way to forget my worries is chips and cheese, and that I need to be stuffed before I go to bed. These requirements are just thoughts, aren't they? By labeling them, they somehow have become less powerful. I'm not their slave anymore. I can go to bed hungry and say to myself, 'I'm hungry,' when I feel my belly rumble. It sounds simple, but it's a revelation: I'm in control now!"

Six months passed, and Robin called me to let me know that the fiftieth pound had come off. Thanks to bridging and mind-body mapping, which she continued to do, eating, she said, had become no more important to her than any other part of her life.

Keith, a successful, hard-driving investment banker, reported his experience after just two days of awareness practice. "During a meeting, I tuned in to the air-conditioner noise, and I found that my back was so tight it was painful. Just tuning in to that tight sensation allowed me to relax my back. When I was at my computer later that day and listened to its hum, I suddenly noticed that I was leaning so hard on my elbow that it hurt. It's amazing how much damage I've been doing to my body! Now it's fun to come to my senses and discover that I can be at ease much of the time."

Never underestimate the power of abiding in the spaciousness of your natural, free-functioning self. Remember, the goal of the Identity System is separation. Eliminate this artificial separation 24/7 with the bridging activities described above. Continually return to what is going on in the moment.

Doing bridging practices throughout the day has no goal. You're not striving to be calm or relaxed; that is the fixer talking, always trying to fix something that isn't broken. With bridging, you are present with your surroundings, whatever they are. If you are tense, don't fight it; just become aware it. If you're breathing shallowly, just be aware of that. You do not have to fix anything.

Bridging helps you observe how your depressor and fixer requirements affect your daily activities. With bridging, you become more joyful as your true self has space to breathe, freed from the Identity System's grip. These practices are healing because they reduce fear, anxiety, and tension. Like a very young child, your awareness is expanding, returning you to your natural self, where the possibilities are endless!

Specific Bridging Exercises

Try one of the following bridging practices each day of the week. The secret is consistency.

- *Background sounds.* Briefly and frequently tune in to the sounds around you. This easy exercise has surprisingly strong impacts: It nourishes your body, mind, and spirit and connects you to the world around you.
- *Bodily sensations.* How does your stomach feel, your back, your neck? What points of your body are pressing on the furniture you're using? How does your shirt feel on the back of your neck? Is your waistband too tight? Pay attention to your body: it is sending you signals all the time. Your awareness alone is enough; understanding the signals is extra.
- *Coming to your senses.* What do your fingers touch? Be aware of those sensations. Do you feel the heat or sun on your body, the breeze on your face, the tightness of your clothing, the hug of a loved one, the handshake of a new friend? Do you really see the old tree in your yard? Do this kind of thoughtful inquiry for all your senses.
- *Recognizing Channel Me.* This channel features your daily dramas and storylines—your pet peeve, your daily escape to la-la land, your financial concerns, or your family problems. Be aware that these thoughts and storylines bulk up your Identity System and mask your true self. Notice them, acknowledge them, and then move past them by returning your attention to whatever task is at hand. When you turn off Channel Me, you turn yourself onto life.

Self-devised Awareness Practices

Once you understand bridging, your own life will present you with opportunities to design your own practices. Angela was a young single mother whose daughter, Serena, at six years old, had become unmanageable—screaming, arguing, and throwing tantrums. Angela was at a loss. She would come to my parenting workshop and leave Serena in the childcare facility down the hall. Frequently, however, Angela would be summoned by the childcare providers to calm her screaming daughter.

Angela developed a strong bridging practice and, almost accidentally, invented her own personal and extremely effective form of bridging. One evening Serena threw a terrible fit, and Angela had to rush down the hallway and whisk her to the bathroom. We could hear the screams increase in intensity and volume. Suddenly, they stopped. We all held our breath, waiting for the return of the tantrum, as was the usual pattern, but the silence continued. A short while later, Angela quietly reentered the room. She had returned Serena to childcare. Both she and her daughter remained calm the rest of the evening. At the conclusion of our meeting, another participant asked Angela what had happened.

"I was in the bathroom with Serena, with my hands covering my ears," she said. "It was so bad I thought I was going to start screaming too, but suddenly I began to concentrate on the pressure of my fingers against my head, and somehow it became clear to me that I was *not* a bad mother just because my daughter was screaming. When I realized that, I felt a heavy burden was lifted.

"Then I started to focus on Serena's screaming and saw it in a new light. I could use her screaming as an awareness practice! I just listened to it and watched my little girl, feeling more loving toward her as my anxiety lifted away. I saw my thoughts coming and going and even experienced my body relaxing. Suddenly I had this urge and I picked Serena up. I turned her face to the mirror and said, 'Look!' Immediately she stopped screaming. Just like that! It just happened. I have never done anything like that before."

In the past, Angela's entire being was fixated on the belief that she was a bad mother, and she had let Serena's screaming reinforce that belief. She had perceived herself and Serena as damaged. Her improvised-on-the-spot bridging practice rested her Identity System, normalizing her mind-body connection and giving her space to freely respond to a difficult situation. Angela's entire body and mind no longer held fast to the belief in the damaged self. In fact, this experience was a dramatic turning point in Angela's life. She became more outgoing, her self-care improved, and her inner and outer beauty began to shine through in the remaining group sessions.

Lucien, a seemingly mild-mannered professional dancer, was referred to an anger-management class because of several violent altercations. As a person already attuned to his body, he designed a number of body-awareness exercises. Following are two exercises that he demonstrated for the class and that other participants found useful. Both help to stop and rest the Identity System by relaxing your body and actively expanding your awareness.

Stand and find a comfortable position. Now visualize that you are seaweed attached to the ocean floor. Close your eyes and experience how your body responds to the gentle ocean currents. Imagine the sights, sounds, and sensations caused by the movement of the water. Try this exercise for a few minutes. Be aware, and sense your body moving ever so slowly and gently. If thoughts interrupt, let them go without analyzing them. The practice is just to be present.

The next exercise is to stand with your arms extended to the sides of your body, at shoulder height. Bend your arms at the elbows so your forearms are 90 degrees to your upper arm. Your palms should face down. Pushing slowly down with your palms, exhale. Feel the resistance. When your arms are fully extended down, rotate the palms to face up and inhale as you bring them back to their starting position. Experience the air filling your body with vitality. Continue to do this practice slowly and mindfully for a few minutes.

Dee attended a weekend bridging workshop to help her cope with her chronic tinnitus (constant, high-pitched ringing in the ears). Though she was a successful social worker and was happily married, Dee felt that her life was being disrupted by the tinnitus. Her doctor had advised her that it was untreatable. When she first tried the bridging awareness practice in which you tune in to background sounds, she raised her hand and complained that the ringing in her ears prevented her from focusing on the ambient noise. The next day, however, she returned to the workshop and reported that she felt very fortunate, for she had discovered that her tinnitus gave her a built-in source of white noise to focus on, returning her to the present moment, anytime, anywhere! She had made lemonade of the lemons life had given her.

Driving can consume hours of your life, and for some people, it leads to tension, anger, and depression. Drew was one of those people. As a pharmacological representative for a drug manufacturer, he drove all day from one doctor's office to another. Though he enjoyed the work, he felt burned out by the hours he spent in traffic. He signed up for a two-weekend burnout workshop with me, and by the second weekend, Drew reported that he had begun to enjoy driving. A simple technique he devised alerted him to an active Identity System: At the start of his day, he would set his rearview mirror high enough so that when he was sitting upright he could clearly see out the back window. When his Identity System took over and he began to get angry at traffic, he slouched and could no longer see out of the mirror. This brought him back to his senses, and he would straighten up and drive on, aware that he was spinning off into one of his daily dramas of frustration.

With any awareness practice, the point is not to alter what you do but simply to be aware of yourself as you do it. Sense gravity tugging your feet as you walk downhill, savor the smooth glide of your razor as you shave, enjoy the quiet peace of the moment as you paint your fingernails. Awareness is the key.

All of these techniques bring you back to the moment. They are the first half of bridging. In the next chapter, you'll discover the power of labeling your thoughts. Labeling is part of bridging's second component, which is "Befriending the Identity System." With labeling, you gain a surprising amount of objectivity, enabling you to assess your thoughts and problems with the dispassionate but concerned way you might use to help a friend.

4

Label Your Thoughts and Set Them Free

As anyone who has watched baseball knows, pitchers can quickly go from having a brilliant game to a dismal one. A few mistakes or a teammate's error and a pitcher's mind can become jumbled with concerns, whereupon his body becomes tense. Because his role is a strategic one, a pitcher's busy head often interferes with his natural functioning and hence with his own body's mechanics. In my work with professional baseball coaches, I've taught them how to help their players by resting the Identity System through labeling their negative thoughts. When a game starts to fall apart and the pitcher begins to berate himself with thoughts such as "How come I threw this outside?" or "I didn't release the ball soon enough," labeling these thoughts helps the pitcher come back to what's important: the feel of the ball in his hand, the spikes in the ground, his body moving smoothly on the mound. This awareness allows his body's natural wisdom, seasoned by decades of training, to perfect his pitching mechanics. The thought becomes "just a thought" and doesn't burden his performance.

Labeling a thought is no different from labeling anything else: this person is a senior citizen; that dog is a Dalmatian; this spice is coriander; your car is a sedan. Labels simplify life; they allow us to recognize something and then set it aside, leaving our minds clear for other issues. Labeling thoughts allows you to acknowledge and then set aside your fixer and depressor. Label only thoughts, not physical sensations, sights, or sounds. These do not activate the Identity System as thoughts do. After labeling your thought, return to the moment and what you are doing. If you do not label your thoughts, you are likely to be caught in your daily drama, giving your thoughts room to spin. The more you interrupt your Identity System, the weaker it gets.

For instance, as I prepare materials for my classes, I sometimes think, "I wonder if they will understand what I'm presenting." Labeling this thought is just that: "I'm having the thought, 'I wonder whether they will understand what I'm going to present,'" or "I'm having the thought, 'I wonder if my talk will be clear.'" Then I use that thought as a helpful reminder, review my material, and continue preparing. If I had not labeled my thought about my concern over my presentation, I could have developed an unproductive storyline such as "I should have started preparation earlier. I'm tired. This is difficult; I don't need all this stress. Maybe I'll just do it off the top of my head. No, remember how your Pennsylvania presentation didn't go as well as you liked because you didn't prepare enough…" In the meantime, my shoulders would have drawn up, my breathing would become rapid and shallow, and my head would become dull. My task at hand—preparing for a presentation—would have shifted from a dance of my natural functioning to a waltz with my damaged self.

Just the Facts: Labeling Simplifies Life

The beauty of labeling your thoughts is that you come to understand that a thought is just a thought. No more, no less. On the

1960s *Dragnet* television show, the victims or witnesses to a crime would run on and on with extraneous details as they recounted their tale to the police. Sergeant Friday would unfailingly have to remind them, "Just the facts, sir." Labeling allows you, like Joe Friday, to keep your eye on the ball and to screen out all the extraneous, nonproductive thoughts that can clutter your brain. Just keep this in mind: If the Identity System does not hijack your thought, it will not adversely affect you. Soon, there will come a time in your life when every thought will deserve a smile, as the gentleman in the following example would attest.

Anger Management

Bryce was ordered to attend one of my anger-management classes after an incident of road rage. He wasn't happy with himself for always losing control of his emotions, and so he was delighted by the concept that he could label his own thoughts. "I'm going to run that bastard off the road!" became "I'm having the thought, 'I'm going to run that bastard off the road.'" After a few weeks in class, he arrived one day jubilant. He had been on the highway when someone not only honked his horn at him but also gave him the finger. His rage kicked right in, but then he kicked it right out by labeling his thought. And then, he told us, he actually smiled at himself. He smiled, and next he started laughing over the realization that he was no longer a slave to his thoughts. He taught his wife and children to bridge, and from this formerly anger-prone man came this bit of wisdom: "Look at the world. Thoughts are causing all that killing."

As Bryce's story shows, labeling your angry thoughts can bring a surprising inner peace. Deena experienced the same melting away of anger. After an unpleasant divorce, Deena was ordered by the court to attend anger-management therapy. Unfortunately, traditional counseling was unsuccessful. She remained belligerent and uncooperative. Then she was introduced to bridging, and within days she sensed a new peace. Coming back to her body and to background sounds and labeling her thoughts seemed to melt the anger away. She describes her new peace as arriving without much effort: "It is sort of like a flock of birds just flies away with my thoughts."

Kate ran a successful small business but had a very unsatisfactory relationship with her husband. After a week or two of bridging, she reported to the group that her husband had asked her to go on a vacation. Her first thought was, "What a jerk; we can't get along for two hours! How can he suggest a two-week vacation?" In the past, she would have immediately voiced this thought, and another fight would be on. This time, however, she gripped the table hard, sensed the pressure on her fingertips, came to her senses, and labeled the thought before speaking. "No, I don't think so," was her mild reply, and the matter was closed. Labeling didn't immediately solve the problem of her unhappy marriage, but it provided a conflict-free zone, a place in which communication might lead to a happier state. More important, Kate sensed a new calm in her life that wasn't dependent on how her husband acted. She was able to reduce her blood-pressure medication and begin sleeping through the night, a pleasure that had long eluded her.

Addiction

John, twenty-five years old, had a strong religious background, but had started using alcohol and drugs as a teenager. Despite intensive outpatient and residential treatment, he had been unable to remain free of intoxicants. After five years of treatment failures, he was introduced to bridging in an inpatient setting. After successfully completing his treatment, he wrote to me,

> At first, I was skeptical. The terminology surrounding the Identity System is very secular. I was wrong. It is all based

on us and on our connection with God. Labeling thoughts and coming back to background sounds is so simple. I am glad I dropped my pride and embraced this new way of experiencing my life. Bridging the Identity System has brought the Holy Spirit and peace of mind back into my life. Your simple tools make sobriety possible. Thoughts are just thoughts. Thank you for this wonderful gift!

Jennifer, the director of a treatment facility for chemical addiction, treated John. His story of addiction was not unusual. She told me that nearly every client she works with seems stuck because they carry so much guilt and shame from their addiction. They feel worthless, contaminated, and diseased. For her clients, there was a paradox: while she wanted them to understand that they were not damaged or broken, she also wanted them to remember the mistakes they made while under the influence and how horrible they felt when they went against their own value systems. This memory, she believes, is important to prevent relapse. The challenge, she found, was to have clients remember that their actions have caused pain while simultaneously internalizing the idea that *they* are not damaged.

The knowledge of the Identity System made her job, and her clients' lives, much easier. Now when she counsels her clients that their damaged self is not who they are but is merely a product of their Identity Systems, they begin to see their own power. They begin to realize that the thoughts which burden them and create the damaged feeling are only thoughts. Bridging helps take them from a place of tension, frustration, and self-hate to a place where they experience the peace, love, and acceptance that is always available from their Source. They learn that the power is within them, not located in any one particular place or achieved through any particular self-improvement regimen.

Indeed, Jennifer's own life changed with her thought labeling and bridging: "I used to think that I needed to go to the mountains and sit on a rock to feel all of the beauty and wonder of God's creation. When I rest my Identity System with thought labeling, I can find that feeling from my Source at any time and in any place. Now I don't have to remind myself that I am not damaged or broken and that I am exactly as God created me."

For Frank, labeling thoughts and returning to his body's sensations through bridging allowed him to finally begin the long climb out of addiction. After an intervention by family and friends had put the spotlight on the deterioration of his real-estate business and family life, Frank sought out treatment for his abuse of alcohol. He came to one of my bridging classes and reported that he was drinking to ease tension and anxiety. When he wasn't drinking, he said he felt a "total body aggravation." He even had a term for this condition: the "mumbles." When the mumbles came on, he sought to quell them with drinking. If he didn't drink, his mind would be filled with self-deprecating thoughts and his body felt tightly wound and agitated.

During Frank's second session with me, he seemed very uncomfortable and said, "The mumbles are here." I asked him to listen to the fan noise coming from the room's heater. After a minute or so, he reported that the mumbles were absent when he focused on the sound. He was astonished that the mumbles ceased. I related to him that the mumbles were simply the bodily motor of the Identity System and that his self-deprecating thoughts were the Identity System's mental component. All he had to do to quiet the motor was label his thoughts, as in "I'm having the thought, 'I'm uncomfortable; I need a drink,'" and come back to his senses (sights, sounds, and bodily sensations). He now had new tools to deal with the root cause of his drinking. With a diligent everyday bridging practice, Frank's entire life began to transform. He was at ease with his family and friends without needing alcohol. He was less driven but more productive at work.

Performance Enhancement

At work, you may think, "I'm not doing this right." Before you get wrapped up in the consequences of that negative assessment, just label your thought: "I'm thinking that I'm not doing this right." This not only gives you space but objectivity: you've stopped your Identity System in its tracks, before it can grab the thought and set off a negative chain reaction—self-blame, tension, anxiety. You can relax and be ready to correct your work, naturally, just as you would if you were helping someone else correct an error he or she had made.

Labeling your thoughts is a performance enhancer. Linda, in her late thirties, was a serious amateur tennis player. She was never able to play up to par because of her busy head. Her state of mind and to-do list on any given day significantly affected the outcome of that day's match. Linda even came to expect it: "Oh, this is going to be a bad day. I have a headache; my in-laws are coming; I have a dentist appointment." These types of thoughts led to the next: "I am going to play a lousy set of tennis."

Bad days and interfering thoughts didn't go away. What changed Linda's game—and her general satisfaction with life— was when she began to label those thoughts. She labeled the thought "I wish I felt better today" and then turned her awareness to the breeze on her face, the call of the birds, the heat rising up from the court surface, and the traffic sounds in the background. She expanded her awareness beyond her thoughts to feel the grip on the racket and the movement of her body bouncing up and down when she was receiving a serve. Before she served, she turned her ritual practice of bouncing the ball twice into a bridging practice. She focused on the ball's fuzzy texture and tuned in to her arm's movement as she tossed the ball down, feeling the pressure on her hand as it returned to her. Her body and mind were relaxed and ready for the serve. She had come to her senses and transcended the interference thrown up by her own thoughts. Another technique she found very helpful was keeping her eye on the ball as it would hit the racket and observing the impact of the ball on the racket rather than immediately jerking her head to see where the ball went. Linda found that by keeping her head down, focusing on the impact just a bit longer than she had in the past, her stroke improved dramatically. When she would get behind in a game, she was able to label her thoughts about her concerns and then continue with the play by coming back to being present in the moment. Even on days with headaches, worries, or a long list of tasks ahead of her, Linda played well. For the first time, she reached the top tier of players at her club. She continued bridging after she left the tennis court, allowing her to handle daily challenges with more calm and less stress.

Readiness for Challenges

Bridging can prepare you for any conflict, no matter how you feel. Walker is a karate instructor who attended one of my bridging seminars. Soon after, he had a tournament match. Unfortunately that morning, he experienced a deep fatigue, brought on by a poor night's sleep. In the past, Walker's fixer would take over in such a situation: "You're going to fight it; you're going to be strong; you don't need to be tired." Now aware of his Identity System, Walker simply labeled the thought "I'm tired." He quickly came back to his body's sensations. He then began the match feeling relatively calm and aware of his body, background sounds, and his opponent's movements. Despite his fatigue, Walker's timing in the match was impeccable, and he was quick, clear, and strong. It was almost as if he was reading his opponent's thoughts and accurately predicting his moves. What was a revelation for Walker was that, by using labeling and bridging, he found he didn't need to feel a specific way in order to perform superbly. He simply needed to expand his awareness beyond his own limiting thoughts.

Though not an athlete, Latanya faced a formidable foe each day in her life. Suffering from multiple daily panic attacks, she was virtually restricted to her house, and because of this, she felt constantly that she was a bad mother and a bad person. Within days of beginning a bridging practice, her formerly constricted life began to open up. She would label her thoughts all day, even innocuous ones such as "I have to go to the bathroom." She became adept at this, easily returning to her bodily sensations, and almost miraculously, she was able to venture out as the panic attacks decreased. Her own fears had receded into the spaciousness of her possibilities, much like how the red water that represented pain in chapter 3 receded to insignificance when it was placed in the largest beaker. Within a month, Latanya's attacks ended. When thoughts arose that she was a lousy mother, she would smile. Sure enough, as she was resting her Identity System more and more in her parenting role, the children did better in their schooling and activities. She herself re-enrolled in college. Latanya reported that she labels her thoughts all day and no longer has to even think to do it. Labeling has become second nature.

As you have seen, bridging and labeling allow you to rest your Identity System thoughts. When you relinquish them as "just a thought," you free yourself to think and act naturally.

5

Befriending Your Identity System through Mind-Body Mapping

Do you have too much on your mind? Like the accumulation of stuff that leads to a messy home, it's easy for your head to fill with the clutter of work issues, relationship problems, bills, self-improvement ideas, and so on. The list is endless. This mental clutter can keep you awake at night, cause illness, prevent you from enjoying time with your family, and even spoil holidays and vacations. The clutter-maker is none other than your Identity System, which spins a mental spiderweb of "must have, should do, how come, why didn't she, it's not fair."

The way to clean out the clutter is to "befriend" your Identity System through the practices you'll learn in this chapter. Like you would befriend a person, befriending your Identity System means that you get to know it, pay attention to it, respect it, become familiar with how it acts, and then treat it appropriately. Appropriate treatment means that whenever you recognize one of the signs of your Identity System (depressor, fixer, storylines, tension, fear, worry, or guilt), you do not ignore it, reject it, or play with it. Instead, you simply embrace your Identity System with your awareness. Anything else is extra. You don't have to control it, understand it, or figure it out. That's all it takes.

A specific practice you'll use to befriend your Identity System is mind-body mapping. Mind-body mapping is taking a question such as "What's on my mind?" or "Who am I?" or even the topic of a recent dream and then on a sheet of paper jotting down sights, sounds, physical sensations, and thoughts related to that topic. Mind-body maps expose how the Identity System works by painting a word-picture of its activity.

Each map takes about five minutes to complete. Mapping is easy and will not only jump-start your bridging practice but will ensure a rapid transformational journey. It revolutionizes the free-association method developed by Sigmund Freud for psycho-analysis, in which a person expresses, without self-censorship, ideas, thoughts, and impressions in order to uncover the under-lying cause of his neuroses. However, rather than years of therapy on the analyst's couch, mind-body mapping helps you in minutes, and its results are apparent within hours. The reason for this vast simplification is the discovery of the Identity System. Although your past does influence the makeup of your Identity System, bridging, unlike analysis, requires only recognition and awareness to rest your Identity System and become unburdened by tension and fears. Once you understand mind-body mapping and its pur-pose, it is entirely do-it-yourself. My use of the term *mind-body mapping*, by the way, is quite distinct from the term *mind mapping* as used by Tony Buzan in the 1960s for a graphic brainstorming and organizing technique used to overcome mental blocks and stimulate the imagination.

Mind-body mapping takes your mind's free associations and the signals your body is sending you and puts them in plain sight on paper so you can see how strong and self-perpetuating your per-sonal Identity System is. You'll quickly recognize the waltz of the depressor and fixer orchestrated by the damaged self. You'll see details of how your Identity System requirements sustain the damaged self. Most remarkably, you can see your Identity System in action, caught on paper, when you map. After you do, your life will never be the same. As with any problem, once you're aware of it, you naturally do something about it. If your car has been getting poor mileage, for example, you might try to fix the situation by getting a tune-up or by driving less or by driving more slowly to conserve fuel. These things might help a bit, but they haven't addressed the real problem: a leak in your gas tank. Once you expand your awareness to recognize the gasoline spot on your driveway, you naturally do the right thing: you take the car in to the mechanic to repair the leak. Likewise, mind-body mapping helps you recognize the real cause of what has been secretly sapping your vitality.

The picture that each map paints of your Identity System at work is worth a thousand words. The Identity System can hide indefinitely in your mind, but it can't hide on paper. With your first map, you'll experience the start of your transformative journey from an Identity System–driven self to your true self.

Closing the Open Loops Spinning in Your Mind

Your Identity System makes use of open loops, which are thoughts that demand attention or require action. Open loops occur in any type of system. In a home heating system, for example, an open loop is created when a room's air temperature drops below the temperature set on the thermostat. A sensor detects the low temperature, thereby signaling the system to close that loop by turning on the heat. If the temperature rises above the thermostat level, another open loop is created. The system senses this open loop and turns off the heat. Systems respond with an action each time an open loop is created.

When open loops occur in the body's systems, a body-mind function is activated to close it. An itch is an open loop that prompts a scratch. Scratching alleviates the itch, thereby closing the loop. A "natural open loop" is one in which the action closes the loop and leaves no trace. A "dysfunctional open loop" occurs when the action does not close the loop. If the itch is caused by a mosquito bite or allergic dermatitis, you scratch but the itch returns—a sign of dysfunction. Both of these loops are shown graphically in the Natural and Identity System Functioning diagram in chapter 1.

Open loops in the mind are a natural manifestation of our busy lifestyles; the more you put on your plate, the more you create open loops that require you to act in order to close them. In addition, your mind often spins with open loops because you do not always think of tasks or problems at a time when you can take the appropriate action to close the loop. For example, you might think of cleaning the attic while you're at your job or while vacuuming your house in preparation for guests. If you have no time to actually clean the attic when the thought arises, then "I need to clean the attic" stays in your mind as an open loop. When you eventually clean the attic, the loop closes.

It is natural for open loops to come and go spontaneously at any time. The free-functioning mind is open, ready, and relaxed and is constantly solving problems by presenting you with open loops. For example, in the morning, you create an open loop by asking yourself what you are going to wear today. Your mind solves the problem by choosing an outfit and by directing the actions that enable you to get dressed. That is natural functioning. But even such a simple question of what to wear can get hijacked by the Identity System if, while driving to work, you ruminate about not having the proper suit on for a big meeting or being overdressed for an interview. The Identity System loves open loops, and once it locks onto one, you are in for quite a ride.

The "To Do" Map

Let's look at how to close some of these open loops. We'll do this by creating a "To Do" map. Take a blank piece of paper, draw a small circle in the middle, and write "To Do" in the circle. Take a few minutes to jot down thoughts that arise about things you need to get done. Scatter your thoughts around the paper rather than listing them in a linear arrangement.

Take a look at Elliot's "To Do" map, which follows. He has lots of open loops cluttering his mind—"Pay cell phone bill," "Arrange time for gym," and "Clean windows." But not all open loops are created equal. Some, like "Prepare for tomorrow's meeting tonight" and "Call mother," are much more charged with baggage and emotion. These loops are susceptible to Identity System meddling.

On your "To Do" map, put a + sign next to items that make you a little tense and anxious and ++ next to those that make you quite tense and anxious.

On Elliot's map, the open loop "Prepare for tomorrow's meeting tonight" worries him and makes him extremely anxious. Even as we worked together in a business workshop, Elliot felt tension in his neck and shoulders. These are manifestations, both mental and physical, that the open loop had been confiscated by Elliot's Identity System. The result was that he ended up experiencing himself as damaged.

In contrast, when I asked Elliot how he felt about the open loop "Pay cell phone bill, " he replied, "That's no big deal. I'll just write a check in the next few days." Just a kindly reminder. Again, not all open loops are created equal!

When you experience tensions similar to Elliot's about the items on your own "To Do" map, you have just taken a big step in recognizing the presence of the Identity System's helpers, the depressor and the fixer, hard at work to reinforce or repair your damaged self.

Prepare for tomorrow's meeting tonight. ++

Pay cell phone bill.

Clean windows.

Arrange time for gym.

To Do

Start collecting design information.

Call mother. +

Get into work early tomorrow.

Call to get appointment for teeth cleaning.

Elliot recognized that although his previous attempt at preparation for the meeting started out with natural mind-body activities appropriate to the needs of the task, such as collecting, organizing, and reviewing his data, his Identity System quickly jumped in with fear, worry, and self-recrimination. No matter how well his preparation was going, he was still tense and anxious because the Identity System was doing what it does best: perpetuating an unquestioned body and mind belief in a damaged self. Once it takes over, any activities to prepare for the meeting become a series of attempts to fix the damaged self. At that point, no matter how hard Elliot prepares, he can never heal the damage, fueled as it is by Identity System fear.

Resting Your Identity System

Elliot was about to learn that with a resting Identity System, he could simply prepare enough for the meeting to close the natural open loop "Prepare for tomorrow's meeting tonight." He had the skills, the experience, and the materials he needed to make an effective presentation. He knew that; what he had not known before was that his doubts, tension, and fears were not his true self talking to him but his Identity System trying to undermine his own natural and true functioning. Elliot soon got to the point where, whenever he felt the onset of tightness in his chest and the negative self-talk, he could rest his Identity System by tuning in to ambient noise, smiling to himself, and continuing with his work.

In the Identity System, all open loops are dysfunctional. Every requirement the Identity System brings up is an open loop demanding action, but sadly, the action does not close the loop. For instance, an alcoholic has a requirement: to drink. One martini does not satisfy the requirement. Two martinis only increase the intensity of the requirement. No matter how many drinks he consumes, he cannot close the loop because the sole purpose of the requirement is to strengthen the false belief in an incomplete self, which in turn reinforces the requirement.

That is why fulfilling depressor or fixer requirements can never heal the damaged self. When a fixer requirement ("Prepare for the meeting") is fulfilled, the depressor pops up, like a wet blanket, dampening any feeling of accomplishment with thoughts such as "I can't think of any more I can do to get ready for this meeting; I have a bad feeling I missed something," or "I've bought my husband's birthday present, but now I feel that he may not like it."

So, as you've seen, mapping is the way to rest your Identity System and close those pesky open loops. With mapping, you cast an objective eye on your Identity System requirements. Once you recognize them, you can rest them—and get on with your life.

The "What's on My Mind" Map

Take five minutes (but not more) to create a "What's on My Mind" map. This map provides a snapshot of your mind's present activity. It does not have to contain your every thought and sensation. That would be impossible! It would take days to jot down everything that is on your mind during any given five-minute period. No matter; you can write down a surprising array of thoughts and emotions in five minutes, which will be enough to see and experience how your mind naturally reminds you of things to do, screens out countless unwanted stimuli, and holds tremendous capacity.

Get a blank sheet of paper and a pen. The blank sheet represents the vast potential of your mind. After you write "What's on My Mind" in the center of the paper, circle that phrase and then randomly jot down whatever pops into your mind. Notice the great variety of thoughts, sensations, sights, and sounds that bombard you in every moment. Represent these stimuli on the paper with simple statements such as "Hearing traffic sounds," "Seeing words appear on paper," or "Sensing pressure on my sitting bones."

When you're done, the transient scenery of your mind over the past five minutes has become a fixed tableau of words, phrases, and sentences. Each moment, your mind has a single set of contents—only to have a new set the next moment. Thoughts are birthed in an instant, hundreds born in a blink of an eye. However, to retain and recognize them, the contents of your mind need to be printed out in real time. Hence the map. Even this limited record of a fraction of your thoughts is very helpful in getting to know how your mind functions and in coming to recognize what is interfering with its free functioning.

Following is Deedee's "What's on My Mind" map. You can see the simple and direct statements that naturally take up space in her head. By just looking at these statements, you can begin to distinguish between Identity System clutter and the workings of a natural, open, active mind.

When Deedee made her map, she said that she felt her mind was full of "junk." I pressed her as to what she meant, and this conversation ensued:

Deedee:	"Many of the thoughts I wrote on the paper are repetitive and troubling. They seem to take up lots of energy. Others are no big deal."
Stan:	"Tell me more."
Deedee:	"Well, definitely the thoughts about work: 'Hate to go to work tomorrow' and 'Won't do me any good to ask for a raise.' Just mentioning these thoughts again makes me anxious and makes my throat tighten."
Stan:	"Those thoughts have been taken up by the Identity System and are being fed into your fixer-depressor cycle, reinforcing your sense of damage. Look at

Deedee's "What's on My Mind" Map

Can hear others writing.

Looking forward to weekend.

Get a baby-sitter and go to the movies.

Would like to go for a hike with Georgia.

Nice painting on the wall.

What's on
My Mind

Maps are easy.

Seat is hard.

Hate to go to work tomorrow.

Seems like I've been here a long time.

Won't do me any good to ask for a raise.

another thought on your map. How does the thought 'Seat is hard' make you feel?"

Deedee: "It's neutral, really. I don't feel much other than my butt on the hard seat."

Stan: "The thought 'Seat is hard' is inherently no different from the thought 'Hate to go to work tomorrow.' Our mind produces a thought whenever certain cells in our brains secrete a tiny droplet of neurotransmitter. That's all a thought is: a biochemical process. The only difference is that one thought has been captured by the Identity System and the other hasn't."

Deedee: "So eventually I'll be able to catch the Identity System before it catches me! Then a thought like 'Hate to go to work tomorrow' won't be as charged, and I won't be as anxious."

Stan: "You can still have anxious thoughts. We all do, and we'll continue to have them, but when the Identity System is resting, we can simply label the thought— 'I'm having an anxious thought'—and move on to the next thing. Remember, we're not trying to stop our thoughts. That's impossible. We're simply being as natural as we can."

Deedee: "I'm getting it—rest the Identity System and I'll be able to take care of my life."

Look at the "What's on My Mind" map that you created. Which of your thoughts are more prone to Identity System interference? The key when looking at your own map is to recognize tension or anxiety associated with a thought and to see if you are registering any uncomfortable feelings. As you create more maps throughout this book, you'll begin to see a pattern and the recurring themes and places where the Identity System interferes with your life. The more you familiarize yourself with your own tendencies through mapping, the easier it becomes to recognize when the Identity System is at play. Although the maps may appear simple, they can become an awesome force in transforming your life. Understanding Deedee's map is a fine start, but it has minimal transformational value relative to creating your own maps.

It is helpful to do a "What's on My Mind" map when you are having trouble or feeling poorly. It renews your sense of the spaciousness of your mind and clarifies how the Identity System—and not outside events—is limiting your life. Kyle, a CEO, phoned me to share how his life had been transformed by bridging his Identity System. He had gone from depression and hopelessness to a full life at home and work. He had developed a habit of creating multiple brief "What's on My Mind" maps every day. Even while on a hiking vacation with his family, he mapped. During a break after a particularly rewarding morning in the wilderness, he looked at the map he had just created and smiled at the item "All days should be like this." Kyle immediately recognized that this seemingly innocuous thought was a fixer requirement; it in effect rejected his ever-changing life. It subtly tried to tell Kyle that there is a particular picture of how his life should be: fun, calm, and peaceful, just as when he's in the wilderness. With this requirement, when he returned to his everyday life, he would not be able to appreciate life and would become tense, anxious, and resentful whenever his life failed to live up to his picture. With mapping, Kyle was able to smile at himself and transform his life, fully appreciating the space he was in.

Kyle's story illustrates another point of how the Identity System can take you out of the moment by creating a separation between you and time. How often have you said, "I'm wasting time," "Time is passing me by," or "I don't have enough time"? Time seems to be something elusive, hard to hold on to, hard to keep track of. Do humans stand helplessly at the station as the time train chugs heedlessly by us, or are we passengers on that train, our souls inseparable from time itself? A mapping and experiential exercise will help answer that question.

The Time Map

On a blank piece of paper, draw an oval in the middle and write "Time" inside it. Now take a few minutes to scatter on the paper whatever thoughts come up about time. Next, become aware of your body's sensations associated with each item you wrote down. Note the telltale signs of your Identity System at work (depressor/fixer activity, anxiety, self-recrimination, and tension). If your map is cluttered with regretful thoughts such as "I lost my youth," "I wasted my life," "I don't have enough time to get things done," or "I'm running out of time," your awareness is contracted, and your natural functioning is impaired. Your Identity System is activated, making you experience a separation from time. Conversely, when your Identity System rests, time is inseparable from you. This contrast is similar to situations when you are bored versus situations when you are engaged. When you are bored, time exists and is creeping slowly by; your Identity System has you waiting for the moment to end, separating you from your surroundings and keeping you self-absorbed. In contrast, when you are engaged in an activity that interests you completely, time seems not to exist. It passes in an instant or seems not to have passed at all, as you and your activity are one with it.

Here's an experiential exercise that allows you to better taste your relationship with time. After reading the following paragraph, put down the book, close your eyes, and tune in to the white noise in your surroundings for a minute or two. As you do, study your mind to see if you can observe the passage of time. Does time pass you by? Are you missing anything? In my workshops and classes, most participants were astounded that while doing this exercise they could not experience time passing by. Those participants who did experience time passing them during this exercise were those who had reported regretful thoughts about letting their lives slip away from them. Their Identity Systems were active, and they could not experience how fully connected they were to their life, to time, and to the Source of all existence. If that was your situation, try the exercise again. Come back to your senses and label your thoughts. Are you on or off the time train now?

Note how when your Identity System is active, you have the requirement, like Kyle did, that life should be better. You reject the moment, and life becomes filled with regrets, disappointments, bitterness, and resentment. Your search for greener pastures nurtures only your damaged self. By being in the present moment (sights, sounds, bodily sensations, and thoughts) you come to appreciate that your higher power has given you a precious jewel—the gift of the moment.

Mapping and Trapping Your Depressor

It's time to create a Depressor map. This map will familiarize you with one-half of the Identity System's team. Many of us tend to push away the depressor's negative self-talk; however, seeing it on paper will be like a breath of fresh air. This map will give you the ability to recognize your unique depressor activity. For one person, it may be "My hair is blah; my complexion is poor; I'm not outgoing enough." For another, the depressor manifests as "I'm too short; I don't have enough discipline," and for another, the storyline could be something like "I'm not quick enough; my mind is too slow." When your expanded awareness embraces such a thought, you have unmasked your depressor, and you can smile as the negative thoughts appear and then disappear.

The Depressor Map

Take a fresh piece of paper and write "Depressor" in the center circle. Randomly jot down on the paper whatever thoughts or physical sensations come up. Often what you write will make you feel bad, or you'll wish for more positive things to think about, or the thoughts will be all too familiar, but just keep at it. All the thoughts and sensations on your map are just natural thoughts and sensations. Negative thoughts are not inherently bad, and you can never rid yourself of them. However, they can make dainty little morsels for your Identity System. Everything on your Depressor map can be captured by it. Remember as you are working on this map that getting your thoughts out of your head and onto the paper is the key to neutralizing them. Take up to five minutes. This map is a bit harder to do than the previous ones because the depressor's job is to make you feel damaged, and the thoughts surrounding that damage are sometimes hard to acknowledge. Stay with it and continue writing down what comes into your head.

When Carla completed her Depressor map, she complained that she hated the feelings it evoked. "Anyone who has these thoughts must see themselves as powerless and damaged. The thoughts 'Can't depend on anyone,' 'Miserable,' 'Depressed,' and 'Little' give me a bellyache. They make me mad," she told me. Her response is normal, but these difficult thoughts are a sure sign that the Identity System's depressor cycle is in high gear. These "negative" thoughts are a road map back into Carla's natural, free-functioning self. Carla soon came to appreciate that all the thoughts on her map were "just thoughts." Whenever they subsequently reoccurred, she would recognize them and smile at herself in relief, knowing that she was no longer drawn in to her Identity System's vicious cycle. If she started to dwell on them, she would label the thought and then proceed with what she was doing.

Look at David's map, which follows. Notice how he lists physical symptoms—"Tense," "Head tight," and "Stiff neck." His Identity System commandeers normal, everyday body aches and pains. Rather than being a free thought or bodily sensation, the ache,

Tense.

Can't control anything.

Afraid.

Don't do things right.

Head tight.

Stiff neck.

DEPRESSOR

Inadequate.

Failure.

Bad.

Unprepared.

Disorganized.

Carla's Depressor Map

Helpless.

Foolish.

Weak.

Can't do things.

Little.

Alone.

Depressed.

DEPRESSOR

Mad.

Miserable.

Stomachache.

Unloved and unattractive.

Can't depend on anyone.

pain, negative thought, or unpleasant event becomes a confirmation of his damaged self.

David may not consciously be aware of the thought "I'm damaged" and may even deny that he sees himself as damaged, but his body is completely convinced. David is now identified with the damaged self. Any time he has the thoughts on his Depressor map such as "I'm disorganized," his Identity System exploits the thought, creating anxiety and tension, thereby reinforcing his false belief. Free thoughts spontaneously come and go, whereas requirements are tied to a system and cannot come and go freely. They are fixed into his personal storyline. The Identity System attaches to pain, discomfort, and misfortune and becomes very powerful.

When David began mapping and bridging work, his Identity System had him coming and going. He either identified with or tried to push away any naturally occurring negative thoughts. However, through consistent work and awareness he learned to understand and gently befriend the activities of the depressor. Now those unpleasant physical sensations that appeared on his map serve as reminders to change his posture, take a short break, and drink some water. They no longer confirm his sense that he is inadequate.

After David mapped the depressor's influence, its effect on him lessened dramatically. Now when he has a thought like "I'm not doing it right" or "I'll never do it right," he recognizes the thought and uses it as a helpful adjunct to his work, spurring him to try another tactic or get a co-worker's help. This is natural functioning. He has created space to bridge beyond the body-mind belief of "damage." This expanded space is none other than his true self.

If, like David, you experienced yourself as damaged as you reflected over the items in your Depressor map, try the following exercise. It's designed to let you experience how false this sense of damage is and to show you that you are whole and complete, despite your very real worries and concerns. First, take a moment right now, close your eyes, and listen to background sounds. Experience the calmness as you focus on the sound. Next, search inside yourself to find where you are damaged. Did you find any damage? If you answer yes, recognize that your sense of damage is due to your Identity System using thoughts about painful events and/or unpleasant bodily sensations to fool you into believing you are damaged. As Julie found in chapter 1, even childhood abuse, as horrific as it is, cannot damage a person if she lets go of these thoughts captured by the Identity System. Your mind has an immense capacity to heal. Rest your Identity System, and it will heal. Don't try to forget about the thoughts that trouble you; just be aware of them, and let them fall into place as nothing more than a small part of your whole, true self.

Unlike David, whose sense of damage came and went depending on his workload, Marina, the wife of an abusive alcoholic, felt that she was permanently damaged. After creating her Depressor map, she was not surprised to see all the negativity on it. When she did the experiential exercise above, she reported that she had indeed found the damage, evident in her thoughts: "I'm not good enough. I cause him to drink. I am not a good wife." I told her that these were just thoughts. On repeating the exercise, she smiled and said, "I couldn't find the damage." With the realization that the damage was a false construct of her Identity System and with the bridging practices of coming back to the present moment, she was able to sleep better, to be assertive, and to set rules for her family without guilt. She became much more active in her home life. Her physical symptoms of constipation, headaches, and backaches gradually disappeared. She gave her husband an ultimatum and he sought out treatment.

Samantha, a thirty-year-old mother of two, had suffered severe brain damage when a drunk driver hit her car head-on. She was hospitalized for months and, after three years of intensive treatment, was irritable, depressed, and unable to handle daily life. She could not get over thinking of herself as irreparably damaged. A friend suggested she attend bridging classes, where she did the experiential exercise of looking for the damaged self. When Samantha opened her eyes, she reported seeing a string of thoughts documenting her physical and mental limitations. She even had with her a pre-accident photograph that showed, she felt, how damaged she was now compared to her old self. I acknowledged that she did indeed have scars and disabilities, but I noted that even while these disabilities were life-altering, they were physical manifestations of the collision and were not capable of changing the absolute value of the woman named Samantha. After explaining about the Identity System's use of her thoughts to reinforce the false sense of damage, I invited her to try the exercise again, searching the vastness of her mind to bring me evidence of her damage. She could find none. Her outlook improved as she saw that her disabilities, while real, did not make her less than she had been before her brain injury.

Eve, an attractive twenty-five-year-old flight attendant, did a Depressor map and started sobbing as she saw on paper all her negative self-talk. She said, "I never knew I was so self-condemning, so damning of myself. It never occurred to me; I never paid attention to it." With awareness of the activities of her depressor and with coming back to her senses, her depression lifted, and some of her friends were wondering if she had gotten a face-lift because her appearance had changed so dramatically. Her long habit of dating married men and "losers" became apparent in further mapping, and she began enjoying being with herself.

Putting a Fix on Your Fixer

The fixer map shows another strategy the Identity System adopts— that of fixing the damaged self.

The Fixer Map

To make this map, write "Fixer" in the center circle of a new page. Let any thoughts about how to improve your life rise in your mind. In short phrases, randomly scatter these ideas on the page. Note the different energy level you have as you write the Fixer map compared to when you created the Depressor map. (If you have not created these maps, please do them now. The few minutes it takes can transform your life.)

If your Depressor map was easier to create, your Identity System has you more locked into a depressive identity and believing its damage myth. Your storylines have you convinced that your problems are due to being injured, abused, neglected, unloved, misunderstood, and so on. This is untrue. It is impossible that anything, except for your own Identity System, can separate you from the source of goodness.

If your Fixer map came easier to you, join the club! For many, creating this map is a far more pleasant experience than making the Depressor map. When the fixer is at work, endorphins flow, because on an evolutionary level, our fixer enabled us to survive. Imagine caveman Og, with an active depressor, sitting in his cold cave and weaving a story about his misfortune: the fire is out, the wood is gone, and game is hard to find. Life is tough, he thinks. Yes, and with an attitude like that, it is probably going to be short. Ab, living in the cave next door, has a strong fixer that spurs him to leave his cold cave, sharpen his spear, order his offspring to gather wood, and set off with determination to spear a boar.

Does your Fixer map give you a sense that you are being driven or that enough is never enough? How do you feel when you fail to live up to your fixer's demands? Compare your fixer and depressor maps. Is your fixer trying to remedy some of the items on your depressor map? Every single item on your fixer map could be natural functioning and lead to living your life at its best. However, if your Identity System captures those thoughts, then they will support the damaged self.

On Carla's map, the items could be natural thoughts of self-care and improvement. However, in the workshop it became clear that the items had become fixer requirements of her Identity System. How could we tell? Let's look at one of Carla's fixer requirements: "Be independent." She said that she believed she could never be independent enough. When she had thoughts about being dependent on others, she reported that she always berated herself and had a sick feeling in the pit of her stomach—an experience of the damaged self. After creating her Fixer map, Carla recognized that requirement for what it is. From this point forward, when thoughts arise which challenge that requirement, such as "I'm weak; I'm needy," she appreciates them as just thoughts. Her striving to be independent has been freed of the yoke of the Identity System. It is no longer a requirement. Carla came to see that her depressor thoughts of being weak and needy were driving her fixer requirement of independence. The fixer always has pleasant packaging wrapped around an unpleasant gift.

Consider some items on David's map that appear positive: "Strive for excellence" and "Please Anita." He reports that no matter how hard he strives to achieve these goals, his thoughts mirror those on his Depressor map: "Don't do things right," "Inadequate," and so on. He never experiences himself as successful or a good husband. Enough is never enough.

Both Carla's and David's Fixer maps include exercise. Nothing wrong with that. "Exercise" is originally a wonderful, helpful, free thought. David asked, "When is a thought to exercise not under the influence of the Identity System? I sit at my computer for hours at a time. What if the 'exercise' item on my Fixer map simply reflects my need to balance all the sitting I do? It may not be anything more than that."

Carla's Fixer Map

Get better job.

Get baby-sitter twice a week.

Be independent.

Don't depend on anybody.

FIXER

Have money.

Be strong.

Have good friends.

Go to beauty salon each week.

Eat right, dress right, exercise.

David's Fixer Map

Take vitamins.

Please Anita.

Do not eat fatty foods.

Get massage and get exercise trainer.

Complete course for MBA.

FIXER

Know beforehand what I am getting into.

Plan ahead.

Be prepared.

Strive for excellence.

Think positive.

Good question! Are self-improvement ideas all futile? Are we simply being manipulated by the Identity System when we try to reach our goals or when we are listening to our bodies and feel that we need to exercise? David's question hit the nail on the head. The purpose of bridging and mapping is to ensure that a cigar is just a cigar, i.e., that the uncomplicated need to exercise, in this case, remains pure, direct, and simple. The way to accomplish this is to have your awareness, embodiment, discrimination, and judgment function naturally. Then you can readily observe when the Identity System is tainting your activity. Most self-help methods suggest what activities are beneficial to you. Bridging is based on faith and trust in your own natural functioning. Bridging is also realistic enough to know that sometimes we are not functioning at our best, and the reason is not that we are deficient but that our best can be corrupted by our Identity System. By learning as much as you can through mapping, "exercise" will be nothing more than that—just exercise.

Many of us commit to improve ourselves with exercise and then fall off our commitment within a few weeks. Quitting the exercise regimen then becomes a victory for the damaged self. The depressor thrives in your struggles, and you keep the damaged self safe and secure. On the other hand, if the fixer is more energetic, you are driven to exercise in order to heal your damaged self. Then, rather than naturally exercising to give your body a workout, the exercise requirement "I need to work out" becomes a dysfunctional open loop that you cannot close. The fixer will inexorably drive you to have a hard body. The depressor responds, "Not hard enough," and you become caught in the Identity System's vicious cycle. Even if you worked out twenty-four hours a day you wouldn't be satisfied with yourself. The damaged self would not be healed. We can try to fulfill the requirement, but the cluttered mind and body tension continues. The fixer may be dominating our mind, but the depressor is dominating our body. The Identity System has us coming and going.

Beware the Super Fixer

Quite often when I work with groups, staff members of the facility where I'm working will sit in and do the maps. Once, a staff manager named Lynne came up to me afterwards and said, "That's a really good technique for the patients."

I asked, "How about for yourself?"

Lynne scoffed, "Oh no, I don't need anything like this. If any stresses come up in my job, when I get home I just run for an hour or so and all my stresses are relieved."

I inquired how she was managing the stresses of that particular day. She said she was actually a bit uneasy because one of the employees had neglected to file an important quarterly report and she was planning to bring it to the person's attention and take disciplinary actions. I asked her how her body felt as we stood there talking about this problem.

She answered, "My chest is tight and my shoulders want to hunch up." Then when I asked her what she was thinking, she answered, "My job is hard. Why can't Michelle [the employee] follow the protocol? What is she going to say when I tell her that I'm going to write this up for her personnel file? Is she going to be mad at me?" She presented a very clear picture of what was going on in her body and mind in that situation.

I suggested to Lynne that physical stress and worried thoughts were manifestations of her Identity System in action and that it might be helpful if she could come back to the background sounds and label some of her thoughts. She reiterated that she didn't need bridging and was just fine handling tension with her evening runs. If she relaxed on the job, Lynne said, she wouldn't get as much accomplished and wouldn't have her high supervisory position—and she said, with finality, that she was not about to "mess around" with her success.

People who are resistant to bridging always interest me. Like Lynne, they're often successful in their lives and feel that resting their Identity Systems would make them vegetables and jeopardize the traits that brought them success. They cling to their Identity System with tremendous power. I refer to these folks as "super fixers"—*super* because their Identity System drives their behavior in a way that enables them to be reasonably adaptive and successful, despite the toll it is taking on them. And yet, inevitably, when I ask these super fixers how they feel after they achieve one success after another, they acknowledge, in so many words, that they don't give themselves any breathing room; their mind just moves on to the next thing, and the next thing, and the next thing.

Often, when these folks do some maps, their Depressor map is usually skimpy and their Fixer map is full of energy and excitement. Their whole day is filled with "to-do's." They need to walk the dog, take care of the kids, spend time with their spouse, take their vitamins, exercise, meditate, work, or do yoga. Sometimes when these super fixers do Fixer maps, they get a real breakthrough accompanied by tears when they see the relentless drive and tension in their lives. They experience what they're doing to themselves. When they note that their Identity System is responsible, a dramatic shift occurs. They feel liberated as they learn how to rest it and finally taste a life without its yoke.

Super fixers' Identity Systems have them convinced that achieving one goal after another is what life is about. They don't acknowledge that within every fixer there is embedded the depressor. As long as the fixer denies the depressor, they feel successful. It seems like the goal of life is just to continue fixing, and their successes let them know they're on the right track. When a goal is not achieved, they just have to work all the harder. They have great difficulty seeing that their lives are the manifestation, the actualization of who they really are.

Thomas, in his mid-forties, is a successful lawyer with a high position in a respected firm and an air of intensity about him.

One of his colleagues had referred Thomas to a series of bridging, labeling, and mapping classes because he was having difficulties in his marriage. Although his relationship with his wife deeply troubled him, throughout his difficulties, Thomas maintained the appearance of power, prominence, and complete control of any situation. He was always at the "top of his game," a super fixer, both at work and in his marriage. His Identity System didn't let his depressor see much daylight. However, his depressor found ample outlet in his visceral personality, as I was soon to find out.

After a number of classes, Thomas arrived one day beaming. I assumed he was going to announce that he and his wife had worked out their differences, but instead, he said, "It's stopped." For the first time, he told the class that he'd been suffering from six to eight bouts of diarrhea each day for nearly eight years. He had tried everything but nothing had worked. His fixer couldn't heal his disturbed gastrointestinal system.

Thomas lacked awareness of his body. By using the awareness practices in this chapter throughout his day, Thomas became open to a new world of sensations. As his body responded to the sense of spaciousness brought by his newly expanded awareness, it healed itself of the bouts of diarrhea. Thomas was no longer held in the viselike grip of his Identity System, and he became more sensitive and open to his wife's needs as well. He was able to address, with his wife, the problems in his marriage rather than try to control them.

Your Unmasked Opponent Is a Friend

You can see that the Identity System does indeed take you down a dead-end road to the damaged self. With mapping, you can observe its strategy of keeping you busy with fixing or experiencing the damage. Once you clearly understand and experience the Identity System's maneuvers as nothing but maneuvers, your awareness is free to expand to transcend the Identity System.

Rejecting, analyzing, or camouflaging it only makes it stronger. You will soon be able to see that the Identity System is not an obstacle at all. It is a signpost and a road map to your true self.

A number of years ago I was on a relatively empty flight. The flight attendant took drink orders, and I was the only one to order coffee. Before it arrived, I went to the restroom and noticed the flight attendant holding a Styrofoam cup of hot water and dipping a bag of instant coffee into it. I asked if that was my coffee, and she said, "Oh yes, sir, it will be ready in a few moments."

Immediately thoughts leapt into my mind: "I paid $350 for this ticket; she's not that busy, so why can't I have brewed coffee? I'm going to demand real coffee. If she doesn't give me brewed coffee, I'm going to talk to the supervisor."

It suddenly became clear to me how I had a requirement: *Stan deserves to have special things*. When Stan didn't get special things, he got hot under the collar; he was damaged. I was so relieved to become aware of that requirement and not have to go through the same scenarios created other times when I felt the service was inappropriate. When she gave me my coffee, I sincerely thanked her, not so much for the coffee but for giving me the opportunity to see a requirement that I was not aware of before.

As my Identity System was resting, I could have easily asked her politely to make some brewed coffee, but I was so thankful at that time that the coffee really tasted as good as any cup of coffee I've had before! Because of uncovering my requirement that I get special treatment, from that point on, my life changed, especially my relationships. Before, whenever I didn't have special things, I'd be damaged and my fixer would demand better. This requirement prevented me from appreciating my life as it is.

Once you become aware of and embrace your Identity System and its various patterns of existence, its power melts, and as your natural connection to your Source is revealed, your true self begins to replace the damaged self and your natural functioning resumes. Growing awareness of the Identity System is akin to sitting around a campfire in the woods, and someone says he sees something moving thirty feet away in the brush. What is it? You become tense and wonder, "Is it a snake, a bear, a cougar?" "Is it poisonous; is it hungry; is it aggressive?" "Should we run?" "Do we need a weapon?"

These spinning questions and fears are the same as those you experience when you function in the upper Identity System Loop shown in chapter 1. If, however, you throw more wood on the fire to create more light, you can see the once shadowy area where the creature is. With the light, you begin to function in the lower Natural Loop, i.e., you can see with clarity whether the animal is a snake, a bear, or simply a branch blowing in the breeze. Awareness naturally expands with a resting Identity System, and then appropriate action follows.

Stages of Everyday Bridging Practice

Everyone's bridging and mapping journey is unique. The more you do, the more you come to grips with the small, specific, everyday items that make up your life. It is awareness of moment-by-moment experiences that actually transforms your life and the lives of those around us. As long as you continue your practice, your perspective will continue to change and develop. You may find some maps more helpful than others. This may well change as you continue to develop your bridging practice and integrate it into your life. The material in this book only has value if it is useful for you.

Following is a brief overview of your everyday bridging practice:

1. The first stage is being able to recognize the signs of your Identity System in action (physical tension, excess worry, fear, preoccupation, impaired functioning, fixer require-

ments, depressor thoughts, storylines). You relieve these manifestations of the Identity System by coming to your senses—the sights, sounds, and sensations in your immediate environment. This shifts you from the Identity System Loop to the Natural Loop, shown graphically in chapter 1.

2. The second stage is when you are able to prevent a free thought from becoming a requirement before you experience signs of an active Identity System. You do this by labeling the thought: "I deserve special things," for example. Awareness keeps a thought a thought, and nothing more—merely a part of your natural functioning. This keeps you firmly in the Natural Loop, and you have a mind that's ready and relaxed enough to deal with any situation.

3. The third stage is when you do not consciously have to make an effort to be aware of or label a thought; bridging happens naturally and spontaneously. For example, if my child is miserable and unhappy, a thought, "I'm not a good parent," pops into my mind. Immediately a light bulb comes on, I acknowledge the thought, and I continue with my parental responsibilities. It's normal, however, even once you reach this stage, to go back and forth between the stages. Remember, your journey through your transformation is unique.

Bridging is your natural endowment. All you need to do in order to claim it is to wake up and befriend your Identity System.

6

Your Search for Who You Are

In this chapter, you'll further explore the world of an expanding awareness that flows from your connection to the Source. You'll compare this bright place with the world of the Identity System. The three maps you create in this chapter, "How I Would Like to Be," "Who I Am," and "How I Got to Be the Way I Am," contrast the polarized world of your damaged self with the unified world of your true self. In our real world, there is no damaged self to heal. Even those aspects of yourself that you want to push away are part of the wonderful whole that is you. Your true self is vast and inclusive of all aspects of your personality; your own natural free function is integrative and not polarizing. Mapping lets you de-polarize your dualistic world and live in peace with the many differences inherent in your nature.

The "How I Would Like to Be" Map

To learn another way to befriend your Identity System and move beyond it, create a "How I Would Like to Be" map. Draw a circle about five inches in diameter. Inside the circle, scatter adjectives and nouns that describe what state you would like your body and mind to be in right now. Use either individual words or two-word phrases. Take two or three minutes and use free association to map this ideal picture. When you have finished, look at each word and put its opposite outside of the circle. Now draw a line connecting each word with its opposite. See David's map, which follows, for an example.

Looking at your own map, notice how comfortably you can embrace all the statements within the circle. They are what your Identity System wants you to believe is your true self. Now take a few moments to dwell upon each item outside the circle. Notice how unpleasant these items are when you attempt to identify with them. This is the Identity System's polarized world. The essential point is not the nature of the contents of the circle; it is the Identity System's exclusion of the opposites. These banished opposites are linked with fear and bodily tension. At the moment you believe your Identity System and refuse to embrace the opposite, you automatically banish your free-functioning true self.

Hal was the founder and CEO of a successful software company. As his company grew, he often had to speak to investors and to civic groups. He disliked public speaking, especially before large audiences, and wished he could work only inside his headquarters, but his company's future depended on his public image. For days before a speech, he was edgy and had trouble sleeping. He described the sensations he felt before each talk as "a big diesel engine revving up inside me." He said that once onstage he fought his way through thoughts of freezing up in front of his audience.

On his "How I Would Like to Be" map, Hal wrote, "Relaxed, open, at ease, good communicator" inside the circle. When he was asked to embrace the opposites of these qualities, he experienced the same symptoms of tension he felt right before giving a

David's "How I Would Like to Be" Map

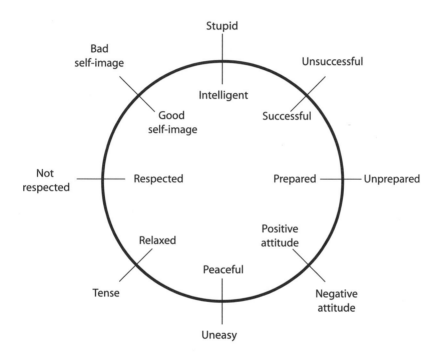

speech, and he asked, "These thoughts are my enemy; why should I embrace them?"

I gently remarked, "You have identified the wrong problem. It is not the thoughts about being tense, closed, ill at ease, or a poor communicator that are the problem. These are merely thoughts and physical sensations. The problem is that when they arise, your Identity System goes into high gear and disrupts your natural ability to function."

The solution is recognizing that when thoughts inside the circle, such as "Be a good speaker," become requirements, the items outside the circle become flash points that ignite your Identity System. Simply being aware of and labeling your thoughts pours cold water over the flash points and rests your Identity System.

Hal immediately caught on. Now before he speaks in public, he no longer fights the adrenaline rush and tense feelings but rather experiences his body's sensations, labels his thoughts, and grounds himself by returning to the ambient noise. By recognizing his requirement—be a good speaker—any thoughts Hal has to the contrary are labeled as just thoughts and do not ignite worry and tension that impact his speech.

In David's "How I Would Like to Be" map, he wanted to be intelligent, successful, prepared, positive, peaceful, relaxed, respected, and . . . just good. These adjectives were within his circle. But when I asked what happened after he had written their opposites outside the circle, he said, "I reject them. I push them away. I don't want to be tense, uneasy, stupid—any of that." David quickly came to see that the more he sought the positive qualities inside the circle, the more he energized their opposite, "negative" qualities. This grasping the good and rejecting the bad fueled his Identity System and increased the mental and physical components of the damaged self. Positive thoughts naturally flow when the Identity System rests. Consciously generating positive thoughts to feel better or deal with a difficult situation stimulate the Identity System and reinforce the damaged self. Rather than countering negative thoughts with positive ones, simply label your thoughts and continue.

Not one of us can function freely if half of our mind is pushing away the other half. Your true self, your freely functioning self, is inclusive of all your qualities and thoughts: the good, the bad, the ugly, the sublime. As you become aware of your Identity System's restrictions by mapping your thoughts and labeling them as "just a thought," your consciousness naturally expands to embrace these opposites. As you shine the light of awareness on your Identity System's activities, its grip lessens and you move from the world of duality into the unified world of harmonious differences.

"Who Are You?" Depends on When You Ask

Don't let your Identity System lock you into the belief that you can be conceptualized as a "somebody," as a fixed self. To experience how your Identity System has you fooled into believing you are a specific, limited "somebody," create a number of "Who I Am" maps over the next week.

The "Who I Am" Map

Draw a large circle on a piece of paper, and inside it list nouns or adjectives that describe your present state of mind. Three minutes is plenty of time. Perhaps early in the morning when the day is fresh and your hair is behaving well, you may describe yourself as "Smart, healthy, attractive." Later in the day, when you have just had a run-in with your boss, you may see yourself as "Dumpy, weak, unattractive." One time it might be "Good energy, meeting commitments, relaxed," and another time "Under pressure, getting behind, stressed." Writing the opposites outside the circle is helpful in breaking the grip of the Identity System.

Once you've created a few of these maps, you can objectively see how you buy into your Identity System's presentation of who you are and how you see yourself as only as good as your last thought. When there are positives in the circle, your entire body-mind experiences these positives. When the circle is full of negatives, your entire body-mind experiences negative states. The Identity System treats you as a yo-yo. When the inside of the circle is full of positives and there are strong emotions and bodily sensations rejecting the opposites, the circle's contents are your requirements—fixers trying to hide the depressors outside. The converse is also true. When the circle is full of negatives and you find it difficult to embrace the positives outside it, your damaged self is feeding off negative thoughts.

Your "Who I Am" map isn't really who you are. It contains just concepts and storylines. It's really a "Who I *Think* I Am" map. Like all the maps you've created, the "Who I Am" map is a gentle method of clarifying what your Identity System is and what it is doing to you. Maps help you become acquainted with your personal Identity System and lessen your belief in its presentations.

The following exchange, played out in one of my workshops, gives an idea of people's different levels of progress in understanding that we are not limited to our Identity System scripts.

Carla: "I've discovered something that may be very important. I've done five or six 'Who I Am' maps, and each is different. One day I wrote, 'Feeling weak, tired, worn out, frustrated, irritated.' Then, an hour or two later, I was writing 'Energetic, optimistic, ready to have fun.' I find it fascinating how much and how quickly my self-image changes. In the past I used to believe that those changing ideas were really me. When I'm bummed out, this kind of mapping really helps. I take my ideas about myself much less seriously now. Before, when something happened, I used to think, drastically, 'Shit happens,' and ruminate about it and feel totally miserable. Now I think, 'It's only a thought.' It's making a big difference. In fact, it's wonderful! I understand why you say, 'Shine your light of awareness on it.'"

David: "I didn't do as well as Carla. I did the maps at different times, like she did, but they were always about 'I'm miserable' or 'I'm miserable but I'm going to fix it.' I see that my depressor and fixer are just taking turns on me. They seem to have me trapped."

Stan: "Your comment on your maps, David, points to a question that could help all of us. Who is this 'me' the depressor and the fixer are working on? Would you say this 'me' is your true self?

David: "No way! It can't be."

Stan: "The Identity System is a master of disguises. The life of the Identity System is dependent on having something to identify with. Because the true self cannot be conceptualized, the Identity System has nothing to latch onto. It will hide itself in anything, in any concept it can present as 'the self.' Its purpose is to prevent your true self from being experienced. Your Identity System has you convinced that you are the damaged self, day and night."

David: "That's right. It does a number on me! It never rests. It's on my case 24/7. If it weren't so sad, it would be funny how it bosses me around. Then, when I try to figure it out, I just go round in circles."

Stan: "You will never figure out the Identity System, David. The 'figuring' only becomes another storyline, with its requirement, masquerading as intellectual help— another fix."

David: "I kind of understand what you say, but I want to know how to work with it. How do I catch it early, before its games begin?"

Stan: "The first step is befriending the Identity System by expanding your awareness to include all of its activities. The space you create in your mind by being aware of them is your true self. Just experiencing without categorizing allows your awareness to expand."

Carla: "Yes, I hear what you're saying. I do feel freer and more open after I see my Identity System working. My awareness may not last long, but at least I know it's there."

David: "I see it, and feel it a little, but I don't think I understand it."

Stan: "The chances are that 'but I don't think I understand it' is again the voice of the depressor, still busily preventing your awareness from expanding. We can easily believe that we really are no more than the concepts mapped out on our 'Who I Think I Am' maps. And we can believe the storylines mapped out on our 'How I Got to Be the Way I Am' maps [see below]. This is contracted awareness, the work of the Identity System, and it can only lead to impaired functioning."

David: "That I can see. I easily start to berate myself about not understanding, and then I become tense."

As Carla and David's conversation shows, getting to know your Identity System and learning the bridging and mapping exercises is not an exact science. Finding your natural free functioning is not a linear process—insights come in starts and stops. One day it might seem an amazing amount of progress is being made, and the next day it might seem hopeless. The key is to persevere and to be as nonjudgmental toward yourself as possible.

The "How I Got to Be the Way I Am" Map

Most of us have pondered the question, "How did I get to be the way I am?" What factors molded you? A favorite teacher, your religion, your parents, family, friends, life experiences? Consider the factors, positive or negative, that were important in your life. On a blank sheet of paper, quickly and loosely scatter the names and the types of these influences.

This map is richly rewarding in that it uncovers how your Identity System creates a false sense of identity by weaving storylines around the items on your map. For example, remember Ron, in chapter 1, whose storyline was that he needed to be twice as good as the next guy? His map listed these factors: "Father drank too much" and "We lived in a bad area of town." This was the long version of his storyline: "If he loved us, he wouldn't have drunk so much; I never had the things other kids had because my father was too drunk to hold a steady job. It's remarkable I overcame that life by working twice as hard as the next guy."

Your Identity System has you believing that you are limited by your own storylines; they become your reality—who you think you are. You become constricted either by wallowing in their misery or basking in their glory. The course of your life becomes directed by these stories, many of which become embedded in your personality traits and physical dispositions. You fail to question their reality, but remember, even if these stories accurately reflected the past, they fail to account for "How I got to be the way I am."

There are no accurate or inaccurate, better or worse Identity System storylines, i.e., a historically accurate storyline is as susceptible to capture by the Identity System as a fantasy. A positive storyline can secure the damaged self as well as a negatively charged storyline. As we saw in Ron's case, a positive storyline of overcoming adversity by working twice as hard as the next guy gave him some solace but still left him with the pervasive feeling of never being good enough. Every storyline that is used to create a limited and limiting identity prevents your free-functioning true self from manifesting.

In creating a life of peace for yourself, do not bother trying to understand or reconstruct the Identity System storylines, for they are just partial explanations of why you are the way you are. Not only are they incomplete versions of your vast, wondrous true self, but they also prevent you from expressing your freely functioning true self. Storylines are the way the fixer or depressor stops you from changing and meeting new challenges as they arise, moment to moment. Even the very effort to understand yourself and clarify everything may be just another Identity System requirement. The Identity System causes you to mistrust your innate goodness and add on something extra: "I need to understand all this." That requirement becomes just another storyline. Only the light of awareness liberates your ever-present free functioning. Be gentle with yourself. Be at peace with your whole self.

Look at your map. Although the items you wrote capture some of the influences in your life, if you wrote for three hours, or even three years, you couldn't capture your genesis. Your true self is so vast and boundless it cannot be grasped intellectually.

The truth is that "How I got to be the way I am" and "Who I am" are incomprehensible. By clinging to fictions about your identity and its origin, you mask your true self and impair your natural functioning. As you shine your awareness on these Identity System activities, you dissolve the web they weave. The Identity System rests, your natural free functioning flows, and you become a person who is fully human, at peace, and in unity with yourself and the world.

7

Living Free of Your Identity System Transforms Your Life and Your Loves

In this chapter, you'll unleash the awesome, unbridled power of your innate natural functioning, free of Identity System interference. You'll use the bridging and mapping tools you've learned about to help you make life decisions and create better relationships.

Natural functioning is also referred to as "free functioning," "integrative functioning," "true functioning," and "pure functioning." *Natural* means that such a way of functioning is inherently present in all of us, like a dog's bark, a cat's meow, or a baby's cry. *Free* means unhampered by Identity System interference. *Integrative* speaks to how this way of functioning harmonizes our body, mind, and spirit. *True* implies that your actions flow from the essence of yourself, not from Identity System–driven notions of who you are. *Pure* implies that our Identity System is resting and that our Source naturally purifies our body's functions, our behavior, and our character. In religious terms, it means that we are doing God's will. (Chapter 10 describes the connection between mapping and bridging and traditional world religions.)

Life is all about functioning: the heart beating; the lungs moving oxygen into the blood; the various glands secreting hormones and enzymes; the kidneys excreting waste products; and the brain perceiving, sensing, thinking, planning, and directing actions. All of these functions are natural, free, integrative, and pure. Most organ systems work automatically and do not require you to direct their activity. However, brain functioning is different. Your brain, the source of your intentions, does have automatic functions such as focusing, remembering, imagining, processing, dreaming, and accepting inputs from the environment and your body. However, these automatic functions have no sense of time or priority; for example, the mind often throws up reminders to do something at a moment when you are unable to do so. If you write down what freely pops into your mind over the next minute or two, you will likely find a hodgepodge of thoughts of varying importance. To reach the highest level of development available to you as a human, intentional activity is essential to complement the automatic activity of your body-mind. Without intentional activity, you would be robot-like and lack the ability to choose and learn from life.

This intentional activity is free will. You cannot survive in this complex, ever-changing, information-driven world without it. Your intentional activity and automatic functioning naturally interact to produce decisions and actions. This is natural, integrative functioning. The only risk to it is the Identity System. While the Identity System has difficulties finding an entry point in your body's autonomous functions because in them all open loops are automatically closed, it finds its opening when intentional activity is introduced. At that point, the loop remains open, awaiting your action. Remember that the Identity System captures open loops and causes them to become dysfunctional. When you cannot close the dysfunctional open loops, the body-mind fills with tension and you experience a deepening sense of incompleteness and failure.

Decision making, i.e., acting with intention, is critical to life. Read on for an example of how to rest your Identity System so you can make decisions unencumbered by its requirements.

Problems Have Natural Solutions

A natural response to a problem can be obscured by your Identity System, as this story shows:

Marion, a sixty-five-year-old retired maid, had created a map about her relationship with her children. She noticed that it was filled with depressor and fixer thoughts, and she spontaneously shouted, "Look! My Identity System is making me a martyr. I thought I was being nice to the kids due to my goodness. But I was being nice because I was being a martyr." When she came back the next week, she told us how this realization had given her an answer to a problem that had been nagging her for years. Several years before, her son and daughter-in-law had borrowed money from her. Now she was living on a small fixed income and needed the money. She had often begun to write letters asking them to repay it, but because she felt proud of her self-sacrifice, she never sent the letters. And they never offered to repay the loan. After creating the map, however, a light bulb came on for Marion: "It is only appropriate that since I need money I need to ask them to repay the loan." Of course, this was the appropriate response, but it was only with awareness of her Identity System that Marion was able to do it. Interestingly, as time went on and as she came to respect herself, her children became closer to her because she was presenting herself now not as a damaged self but as a whole complete person.

In a crisis, when each decision has crucial implications, it is wonderful to know that you have the power to act most appropriately. A resting Identity System gives you that power, as Jane's story shows:

Jane was a regular participant at one of my bridging workshops. She had established a strong bridging practice that helped her deal with the trauma and pain of caring for her terminally ill husband, Martin. One evening, Martin was in severe pain and his breathing became ragged and shallow. She rushed him to the hospital and burst into the emergency room. It was packed, the television was blaring, and children were climbing on the furniture in the waiting room. Jane was told that the ER was short-staffed and that since Martin was not in immediate danger, they would have to wait.

Martin was in agony, distraught by his pain and the commotion around them. She was in turmoil, filled with fear, anxiety, and the feeling of being completed damaged since she was unable to alleviate her husband's suffering. She recounted that her skin was crawling, and every sound—the cry of a baby, the automatic doors whooshing open, the tick of the clock—compressed her anxiety until she felt she would explode. At that point, suddenly, she became aware of her Identity System and recognized that her depressor was feeding her thoughts that she was weak and powerless. She remembered to bridge, and she felt the cold metal of her chair against her arm. With this seemingly minor shift in perspective, her tension lessened considerably. She focused her awareness on the weight of her body resting in the chair, the feel of her feet on the floor, and the sound of Martin's breathing. She noticed with amazement that her spinning thoughts slowed, that her body was more relaxed, and that the sounds which had annoyed her previously were suddenly comforting. Now that she felt more at ease, she was able to comfort Martin and find a staff person to help her move Martin to a quieter place until he could be seen.

When Things Go Wrong

Whatever you do—whether dressing in the morning, cooking dinner for your family, or fixing a lawnmower—is an activity. It may be composed of a single action, or it may be a project requiring a sequence of steps. Each action or each step in the sequence creates an open loop that can be quickly closed by your mind's natural functioning. That is natural problem solving.

But life is sometimes not that simple. There are two ways things can go wrong, and we should not confuse them. The first is when natural difficulties arise, such as an unexpected traffic delay on your way to work, a sudden storm, or a child who gets sick on the day of a picnic. It is impossible to live a life without open loops, without unpredictable circumstances. Natural functioning doesn't mean life will be pain-free and easy; you simply adapt freely and solve natural problems. You close the open loops as you encounter them. The serenity prayer, or Irish prayer, "God give me the strength to change the things I can, the serenity to accept those I can't, and the wisdom to know the difference," beautifully encapsulates natural functioning. The wisdom to know the difference comes from your Source when your Identity System is at rest. The Source provides all of us with a natural capacity to function with clarity, precision, and realistic compassion. When allowed room to flourish, the Source emerges in your actions, speech, and thoughts.

The second way in which things can go wrong is when your Identity System interferes with your natural functioning, when it changes the natural, functional open loops (which leave no trace when closed) to dysfunctional open loops that cannot be closed because the fixer or depressor cannot heal the damaged self. For instance, you may have an Identity System requirement to have everything in your life be meticulously planned and well-executed—a requirement otherwise known as perfectionism. With doubt, tension, anxiety, and confusion, you contribute comments such as "There are too many unknowns; we don't have enough time to plan. Let's reconsider." Your fixer has gotten you angry with others who want a definite answer, and your depressor has you filled with self-doubt and physical tension. Your natural functioning has given you the ability to foresee potential problems; however, the signs of an active Identity System indicate that the damaged self is driving you. When perfection becomes a requirement, free functioning takes a backseat. No matter how many details you fix, others remain. By recognizing your fixer requirement, you can become more effective at planning projects and making decisions. Your ability to foresee potential problems is a gift you can manage instead of it managing you with Identity System–driven perfection requirements. As your awareness of your Identity System grows, your identification with it lessens and you open to a world of new solutions.

Complicated projects or problems with uncertain results are fertile ground for the Identity System. The key to natural functioning is in your hands now: simply be aware of your Identity System requirements and storylines. Sometimes just recognizing the Identity System's interference will enable you to see a resolution of the problem. For example, in one of my workshops, Samantha discussed a problem she had with her nephew, Charlie. As a psychologist, Samantha felt that she should be able to help him deal with his drug and alcohol abuse. She was the only person in the family who would have anything to do with him, but she was confused on how to help him without enabling his addiction. When writing a problem map about her relationship with Charlie, she clearly noticed that her overactive Identity System was giving her shoulder tension and a gripping sensation in her stomach. She recognized her fixer requirement that she solve Charlie's problem, but that night, she still had no idea how to help him. After she slept on it, the next day she decided she would invite Charlie to lunch. When they got together at a restaurant a few days later, Samantha, with help of bridging awareness practices, felt open and comfortable. Without any fixer agenda, she felt closer to Charlie than she had in a long time, and they enjoyed their lunch. A week later, Charlie called her, confided his problem, and asked for a referral.

Resting the Identity System When Making Decisions

In the following example, Susan is at a crossroads. She is searching for a job after having lost hers when her division was downsized. She was having difficulty finding a comparable job. Mapping helped her find one. On her "Get a Job" map, Susan's Identity System has infiltrated the job search, as shown by these items: "I'm eating too much. I'm not sleeping well. My chest is tight and my gut aches." Her depressor is active: "I'll never find a good job." Her fixer wants it easy, telling her that a job should come to her, and her requirements such as "I shouldn't have to look at companies farther than thirty minutes from home" box her in. Even her lack of follow-through after interviews stems from her Identity System's requirement not to look needy. With prompting, once Susan created the map, she was able to see with clarity how her Identity System had been preventing her from taking actions necessary to get a job. Her full awareness and integrative functioning with a befriended Identity System allowed Susan to find a job one week later.

Your Identity System is a master of disguises. A decision may look right, may feel right, and logically may seem right, yet it may be all Identity System. Although we appear to be calm, cool, and relaxed, the Identity System may be in the driver's seat. Decisions that appear too easy or too difficult are often fulfilling Identity System storylines and requirements. An important clue is a history of regret about past decisions and repeated unsatisfactory outcomes. The key is to be open enough to embrace the possibility that your Identity System has been busy.

It is easy to learn to rest your Identity System when you start with simple, everyday decisions. Begin by noticing fixer and depressor activity. Just shining the light of awareness on the decision-making process frees up your natural functioning and gives you new choices. At other times, it is helpful to do a decision-making map.

Finding a job is a bummer.

Need a job with a
fast-growing software company.

I'm not interested in
that job with the
insurance company
that Penny told me about.

I'm depressed.

It should be easier to get a job.

Get a Job

My chest is tight and
my gut aches.
Why did they
downsize me?

I shouldn't have to look
at companies farther than
thirty minutes from home.

I'm eating too much.

I have had possibilities
but I can find something better.

I'll never find a good job

I'm not sleeping well.

The right job is out there;
why can't I find it?

I can't make a good decision.

I applied to Apple but haven't heard anything.
They'll think I'm desperate if I call.

The Decision Map

Decision maps can be used in any area of your life. For the sake of example, here's how to work on a map involving a relationship. Place the decision (such as "Shall I pursue this relationship?") in the center of a blank piece of paper and scatter your associated thoughts and physical sensations around the sheet. Take no more than three or four minutes. As you review the map, be aware of fixer and depressor storylines and requirements as well as the other Identity System signs, such as repetitive themes, fear, telltale physical sensations, and so on. Your openness to all this is your free-functioning awareness, which will allow your decisions to be based on the realities in your life rather than on Identity System fantasies. The map may include items similar to these:

"I need a relationship."

"I need her to be faithful."

"I need him to be honest."

"I always choose the wrong person."

"Am I good enough?"

"No one has ever truly loved me."

"This relationship will give me what I always wanted."

"Without this relationship, I'll never be happy."

Let's assume these themes have come up repeatedly in your life without satisfactory resolutions. When you review your map, you experience anxiety and bodily tension. The expression "I need," whether stated or implied, may well point to a thought being a fixer requirement. If you fail to embrace that possibility, your decision and the subsequent relationship (if there is one) will be based on the false belief that you are not good enough and that your new relationship will fix the damage because it meets your requirements. No matter how faithful or honest the other person is, they will not heal your damaged self. Not having a relationship will also confirm the damaged self. To make things worse, Identity System activity is always associated with decreased awareness, fear, and impaired functioning. You have three strikes against the relationship before you start! Your ability to perceive, appreciate, and understand the other will be tainted and limited by your fear, tension, and anxiety.

Recognizing the fixer and depressor on your map enables you to see how they affect your relationship. This awareness, as always, can break the linkage to the damaged self. After all, it was pure fantasy that you are damaged, and it was pure fantasy that a new relationship can fix the damage and enable you to live happily ever after. The reality is that you are not damaged. The reality is that your relationship may or may not give you satisfaction and fulfillment. Your awareness is so responsive that you will relate more openly and realistically because your feelings are no longer driven by the fixer ("This relationship will give me what I have always wanted") or the depressor ("Without this relationship, I'll never be happy"). Your free thoughts can then encourage you to be more aware and appreciative of yourself and the other.

Transform Your Relationships

As Marion's example showed earlier in this chapter, we all become set in patterns in our relationships. Thus, we narrow down our choices, stifle free functioning, and smother our natural self. To help you make the most of your relationships, let's start by listing your assets:

- You already possess the natural functioning to enable you to dramatically transform all your relationships.
- You now understand mapping and bridging principles.

- You can create relationship maps of the expectations you have of yourself and the important other person.
- You have learned to recognize when your expectations are fixer or depressor requirements.
- You can see and hear, sense your body, and be aware of your thoughts.
- You have the ability to experience the anxiety, bodily tension, restricted awareness, and impaired natural functioning that occurs whenever the Identity System is active.

Thus, you have all the necessary tools to live a free, naturally functioning life. All you have to do is do it. Here's how to transform your relationships:

1. Make a relationship map, scattering the expectations you have of yourself around the paper. Spend less than five minutes.
2. Do a second map scattering your expectations of the other person around the paper.
3. Recognize fixer and depressor requirements.
4. Continue an active bridging awareness practice during the day and pay particular attention when you step on "land mines" (unknown Identity System requirements that cause any anxiety, bodily tension, restricted awareness, or impaired function). If this happens, you will be tempted to react in an automatic Identity System–driven fashion such as getting angry or withdrawing. Immediately, come back to your senses (sensory input, background sounds, and so on) and label your thoughts. Using what you have learned from mapping, see if you can recognize requirements at the moment they become active in your life.
5. You'll be amazed at the new options and possibilities that you become aware of when your Identity System melts. You'll sense a new power and freedom.

The maps of "What do I need from my spouse?" are usually very powerful. In a workshop I held, one man created this map about his wife. He wrote, "She doesn't appreciate how hard I work," "I work all the time," "She spends all my money," and "She should do my job for just a day." He believed that she was causing all of his problems. From his intense physical reaction to the map (his wife was not present), he realized that it was not his wife but solely his Identity System that was causing him to be upset with his wife. After that realization and with the help of a consistent bridging practice, his relationship to his wife changed, and for the first time in years he could now *appreciate* her.

Your old Identity System–driven reactions, based on requirements of the damaged self, can now be replaced by a more expanded awareness associated with natural functions. As you continue to bridge and map, your relationships will be more Source-fed as your awareness expands to embrace the Identity System. Here's an example in the extreme that illustrates the principle:

A colleague on the East Coast uses bridging with his patients. A husband and wife came to see him after the man had threatened his wife and himself. After his wife wrestled the gun away from him, he then took a hunting knife and wanted to stab himself. The authorities were called. After the man was evaluated at a psychiatric emergency facility, he was seen by my colleague, who used bridging techniques to rapidly diffuse the situation. The crisis was resolved and an effective working alliance was created between the couple and the Identity System therapist.

He asked the husband and wife to create a relationship map. With it, they saw how they were experiencing themselves as damaged when their partner wouldn't live up to their Identity System requirements. She saw that she wanted him to be attentive, supportive, strong, and stable and to serve as a fixer for her underlying needs of helplessness and weakness. He was able to see how he was also trying to use her to fix his damaged self. They were able to do a number of maps together, and both actively sought to rest their respective Identity Systems. She became adept at recognizing the signs of her Identity System—such as the knot in her stomach—and found that labeling her thoughts of dependency gave her strength to get past them. He began to use awareness practices—such as tuning in to background sounds—as a mainstay of his life. His self-esteem improved as he recognized that it was only his Identity System and not anyone else that could undermine him. They supported each other in resting their respective Identity Systems.

When you begin to recognize the workings of your own Identity System, you can begin to recognize when it is active in others. Compassion grows. And then when someone is not listening to you, you develop a knowing that she is not consciously shutting you out. Instead, her self-centered thinking automatically restricts her awareness. Her world has become dualistically polarized into inner and outer, and she is drawn into an inner, self-centered existence. In this contracted state of awareness, wisdom, empathy, and compassion are deeply impaired. You have neither to understand her Identity System or to rest it. Your own resting Identity System allows your appreciation of her to grow, and your expanding awareness heals your relationship. Your natural functioning fosters appropriate choices.

Remember, the only purpose of your Identity System is to keep itself going. The Identity System doesn't care whether your partner in a relationship is "faithful" or "honest." The Identity System just wants to keep you busy, to keep you damaged, and to prevent you from experiencing your true self. When the Identity System drives the relationship, it will always drive you to interpret whatever happens in the terms of your depressor or fixer requirements. This will constrain the relationship and ensure that it becomes full of fears, tensions, and anxieties about yourself or the person to whom you are relating. By befriending your Identity System and embracing its activities, these requirements—such as "I need to be honest" or "I need him to be faithful"—can become free thoughts, without fear, bodily tension, or restricted awareness. You will now have available a whole new set of relationship options.

With an awareness of your requirements, even if your relationship takes a bad turn—for example, if your significant other is unfaithful—your free thought "I need him to be faithful" won't trigger your Identity System and awaken the damaged self. While you may experience disappointment, grief, and anger, your true self is larger than these emotions. The spaciousness of it allows for healing much faster than if you were imprisoned by your damaged self. Your damaged self requires him to be faithful to prove that you are lovable; your true self requires no proof, because it has confidence that your natural functioning has the time, energy, and resources to seek counsel from your friends, contemplate your situation, and act decisively. Your expanded awareness creates a knowing which becomes a doing. You will deal appropriately, without ambivalence, with any tough situation, as Rachelle did in this example:

Rachelle had extricated herself from an abusive marriage. At fifty-six, she had divorced the man, but she could not get over him. When he would call to harangue her, she would allow him to continue the verbal abuse, thinking, "It's all my fault; I'm not good enough." Four years of continual therapy hadn't helped her stand up to him. Then her therapist began to teach Rachelle how to use bridging techniques. When creating a map of her relationship with her ex-husband, she saw how her depressor works to lay blame on her and convince her that she is not good enough. She realized that he was not her problem and that by resting her Identity System, she could eliminate her real problem: poor self-esteem. She found it easy, suddenly, when the phone rang, to tell him that she was not going to talk; she was able to hang up on him when he persisted and able to ignore the phone when he made repeated calls. By being able to rest her Identity System, Rachelle's free functioning expanded, giving her a large space in which she is able to live her life and find that "I'm getting over him."

Your free thoughts can help you be more open and responsive to the ever-changing, developing reality of the relationship, yourself, and the other person. You will be able to make natural free-functioning decisions in harmony and balance with your true self while living in reality—whether that reality is picture-perfect or fraught with conflict. Rather than being constrained by fixed and limited needs and concepts, the relationship can develop realistically from your responsive awareness and in harmony with the everyday realities of your life. You will discover the difference between a Source-fed and an Identity System–driven life.

8

Bridging to Peace of Mind

In this chapter, you'll learn a powerful way to gain a new awareness of the spaciousness and the possibilities of your life, opening a door to natural fulfillment. What is pointing the way to this
door? None other than the thing you've come to see as the root
of your problems: the Identity System. In the pages ahead, you'll
see that the signs of Identity System activity are beacons that illu-
minate the path to your true self.

As you now know, the first stage is to rest the Identity System
by coming back to your senses (sights, sounds, and sensations).
Do this whenever you are worrying excessively and are caught
up needlessly in your thoughts. You will feel a calmness and
quietness which confirms that you've successfully created a
bridge to a more wholesome and healthy state of being. The second stage is to recognize the Identity System requirement that is
responsible for catching you up in the Identity System loop.
(See Chapter 1 for the diagram of natural and Identity System
functioning.)

No person or event can ever cause you to experience or express the damaged self. It is *always* one of your natural thoughts that triggers the Identity System, which then transmutes the thought into an unhealthy requirement. Like a bad habit, requirements keep you from living up to your potential. As long as you allow your requirements to remain hidden, your true self cannot flourish.

All it takes to keep your thoughts from being hijacked is to recognize when your Identity System is active and to become aware of its requirements. For example, you might be trying to learn a new skill, such as snowboarding or re-upholstering a chair, where the learning curve is steep. Very likely, when you fall for the twenty-ninth time or make a fatally wrong cut in the fabric, a free thought will likely come to mind, such as "I'm not doing it right." Before you knew how to bridge, your mind might have filled with thoughts like "I should never have tried this," "I'm too old to learn this," or "I'm such a dope!" Shoulders tense, breathing grows shallow, and pressure builds in your chest or head. Your Identity System would bury you in a deep hole, but with the awareness of your own requirements ("I shouldn't have trouble learning new things"), you can rest your Identity System and get past the impasse. Soon, you board down the hill without needing to be evacuated by the ski patrol, or you get that chair covered, to great praise from your friends. You've succeeded!

Never again will you throw raw meat to your damaged self! Now that you know how to bridge, whenever a stressful situation arises and your Identity System rears up, you know how to identify it and politely tell it to get lost. All you need do is immediately label your negative thought: "I'm having the thought that I look like an idiot out here on the snow." This awareness of your thought rests the Identity System, and you can take corrective actions with a ready and relaxed body and mind.

Remember: You are in control. Thoughts are just thoughts. You are no longer limited to being only as good as your last thought. Your confidence naturally rises and your self-imposed limitations vanish. Bridging—this ability to tune in and be fully human, fully alive—is innate, and with practice it will become as automatic to you as saying "Gesundheit!" or "Thank you."

Bridging to Family Peace

The third stage of bridging occurs when bridging becomes inseparable from your everyday activities. Just as an athlete practices his skills every day in preparation for his next match or game, your everyday bridging practice prepares you for the stressful events that accompany every human life. When stress arises, bridging will occur to you as suddenly as a bolt of lightning, as David's story about his relationship with his son shows. Here's how David tells it:

Whenever I get a chance, I try to see how my Identity System controls me. I look for its requirements. Last night, something remarkable happened. My twelve-year-old son, Jimmy, constantly gets on my nerves. He doesn't listen, never picks up after himself, and just thinks of himself and his own immediate needs. He doesn't want to take responsibility. We're not close; in fact, there's a wall between us. The whole family went to counseling last year, and we were taught techniques to deal with our family situation. My wife and I tried and tried to use the techniques of better parenting, like listening, showing interest, and being empathic, but they didn't help. Let me tell you what happened last night. It was like a lightning bolt.

I came home from work, and Anita, my wife, was working late. I was dreading being alone with Sloppy Jimmy. I opened the front door, and lo and behold, his sneakers, socks, and sweater were strewn around the living room. He was playing a video game and he didn't even say hello. I was getting upset and was ready to give Jimmy a piece of my mind and tell him to pick up his stuff and put it in his room.

Suddenly a light came on in my head: I *needed* Jimmy to be neat, clean, respectful, and appropriate; these were my Identity System requirements, and the tension and resentment I was feeling was created by my own Identity System, not by any action or inaction of Jimmy's. I became aware of my jaw muscles, my tight shoulders, and all my lamenting thoughts about my son. As soon as I became aware of my Identity System working, I began to relax. I became open to my thoughts, my bodily sensations, and to Jimmy. I had come within an inch of carrying on in my usual fashion, but I just sat down quietly and observed myself. I read the paper, and then I got myself some coffee. Later, without my doing anything special, Jimmy invited me to watch one of his TV shows with him. I felt a closeness that hasn't been there for years. We talked about the TV program, which I actually enjoyed. I saw that Jimmy has a problem about growing into being a man. I can best help him by not putting my requirements on him.

By creating a problem map, David learned to recognize his requirements. Bridging enabled him to become aware of his requirements, and from that point on, his natural functioning flowed. Our forebearers knew something about the Identity System when they advised us to "Count to ten" when angry or upset. In that critical ten seconds, you can step outside your momentary anger and become aware of the larger picture. In fact, with continued bridging practice, it will happen instantaneously.

Like David, you can let your decisions and actions flow naturally once you befriend your Identity System by labeling your thoughts. Of course, even free functioning and free decision making do not mean that everything in your life will turn out the way you want. Jimmy did not magically transform into a tidy, sociable, and thoughtful pre-teen. However, with a befriended Identity System, David has more freedom in creating appropriate house rules for Jimmy's behavior. He will be more open to Jimmy and better able to see how his Identity System and Jimmy's are active in this issue.

Unlike your Identity System, which demands a specific outcome, natural functioning is not rigidly dependent on a preconceived outcome but is responsive and free to adapt and explore different possibilities. David's annoyance with Jimmy arises when David's depressor causes him to falsely believe that he is somehow damaged when Jimmy's clothes are strewn about the house. Then David's fixer tries to "fix" Jimmy by various methods: yelling, grounding, talking, cajoling, and so on. David's Identity System has one outcome in mind: to reinforce David's damaged self. As David learned, you cannot determine all outcomes, but you can enhance your natural functioning. Your goal and your obligation as a human are simply to be free-functioning at every moment, allowing you to always respond to life situations with immediate responsive compassion and wisdom.

For the matter of Jimmy's behavior, David learned that Jimmy's slovenly habits didn't have to disturb his own well-being. Jimmy has simply presented David and Anita with issues to address. These issues, together with David's and Anita's responses—such as new house rules—and Jimmy's responses give them more opportunities to see how their Identity Systems react. As David continues to befriend his Identity System, Jimmy is given more direction and space to go through his adolescence.

You don't even have to act sometimes; awareness alone changes your perception of a problem, as Tom shows in this story:

Tom and Mike run a large family business with international sales. Tom is the CEO, and Mike is the CFO. The two had often clashed. Mike, though holding an inferior position to Tom, acted as though he was the boss with other employees.

In a bridging seminar, Tom created a problem map centering on his relationship with Mike. As Tom commented on his map, he described many somatic symptoms, including headaches, peptic ulcers, and physical tension. He reported that all day long, even before reaching work in the morning, his thoughts dwelled on Mike and his adverse effects on the company. He sometimes thought more about his relationship to Mike than the company. After doing his map, he saw his requirements about how Mike should be: that he should be a good employee, that he should recognize the boundaries of his position, that he should respect Tom's position.

Tom's face began to relax as he started talking more about what his Identity System's requirements were doing to him. He saw it wasn't Mike's behavior that was troubling him; it was his own Identity System. As he put it, "Mike was only kicking my tires; he couldn't flatten them. The only person who could do that was me, with my own Identity System."

Tom developed a strong bridging practice, and within a few days he reported that his problem was solved. He said it was so simple. Before bridging, he had felt he needed to hold family meetings, revise corporate guidelines, and attend counseling with Mike. "That's all fixer," he said. "All I needed to do was to recognize my Identity System's negative impact, and then my free functioning allowed me to deal well with Mike and the business."

I asked him what specifically he had done to solve his problem. Tom replied, "It was not what I did, it was my being. I was relaxed, open, assured, and didn't waste my time beating around the bush. My damaged self was not in the driver's seat, and Mike knew it." On a return visit a month later, Tom reported that his ulcer symptoms were completely relieved, that he was taking no medication for them, that he was including more recreation in his schedule, and that he was even enjoying the drive to work when he tuned in to traffic sounds and felt the wheel. As a result of having a more relaxed body and mind, Tom's company enjoyed greater success and his health improved dramatically. Mike reluctantly became more supportive.

Bridging to Inner Peace

David's apparent problem was to change Jimmy. Tom wanted to change Mike. Like David and Tom, your Identity System takes your life situations and transmutes them into the limiting concept of a "problem." Mapping is the method that will help you act without Identity System hindrances to actualize your Source each moment through free functioning. When you do that, your problems cease to be "problems." Of course, you will always have issues to address. Make no mistake about that. Life can't exist without them. Illness, relationship problems, natural disasters, and extreme injustices will not go away.

But even hardship and misery are insufficient to dampen your wondrous, expansive, whole, true self, whether circumstances are delightful or difficult, as Phillip's story shows. A professor of philosophy at a major U.S. university, Phillip had been under the care of pain specialists for ten years, having been plagued by injuries, severe tinnitus, diabetes, and acute sleep apnea. To top it off, he was overweight and suffered from hypertension. He had also consulted over the years with psychologists and psychotherapists to help him cope with his existential doubts and fears that, as he put it, "You are all alone; you cannot reach God, and God cannot reach you. When you are dead, you will be forgotten." His Identity System was active: his depressor taunted him with thoughts of "What's the use—you may die in the night anyway," and his fixer urged him to "Start an exercise program and get back in shape!"

On top of this, his mother's prolonged decline and recent excruciating death revived his fears of being powerless. He prayed, "God, I can't tolerate my life as a sick, crippled person. Help me."

In a workshop, Phillip bridged to background sounds. While he was listening, he noticed his tinnitus and his back pain, but as he put it, "Other things required my attention: all the sounds that I had learned as an adult to tune out, the sound of a lady calling for her boy who had wandered off, the sound of autumn-dry leaves blowing on the trees. Those sounds are as real as my back pain. They are happening to other people, like the boy's mother, who doesn't know that I hear her dilemma. My universe has expanded to a limitless degree. The back pain is there, but it has become a much smaller portion of my universe."

Phillip didn't stop there; he realized that when he taught, he was bridging, resting his Identity System. Teaching, for him, brings him to his fullest capacity. When in front of a group of students, he recounted, he is at his most inspired self. He feels closest to God when he mentors a student or writes about philosophy. He said that when he prays, "Father, help me to give my students something of value today," he is inspired, he feels an endorphin rush, and his pain recedes. He is bridging in its fullest sense.

Phillip used mapping to break what he calls the "magic" of the Identity System's hold on him. Once he became aware, through mapping, of its mechanism, sequences, and parts, he can now recognize it when it appears, acknowledging his thoughts and moving on, without letting his Identity System storylines invest his thoughts with any extra weight.

The "Peace of Mind" Map

The "Peace of Mind" map is the most powerful of all the maps you will create, and in my experience, it has led to more immediate transformations than any other map. The purpose of this map is to demonstrate the enormous investment you have in trying to fulfill your requirements. It is to help you see concretely how your Identity System works. The power of the "Peace of Mind" map comes from the fact that it not only maps your individual requirements but also maps how your Identity System operates in the present moment.

This map will be pertinent to many areas and situations in your life. If you apply it to the full range of your life's experiences, over time you'll dissolve the glue of your Identity System, allowing those thoughts that stick unnecessarily in your mind to float harmlessly away.

Let me emphasize that simply following the directions and creating the map with thought and reflection can radically and instantaneously transform your life. Your Identity System melts when you shine a spotlight of awareness on it. Your awareness, as I've said before, becomes a knowing that leads to doing. You have no choice: Your life *must* change, because when you rest your Identity System through awareness, your true self replaces the damaged self.

In the middle of a piece of paper, write "Peace of Mind." Then take a few minutes to think about what would give you peace of mind. As always, write your thoughts randomly around the paper. Here are some examples: "I want to have self-control," "I want to be healthy," "I need to be financially secure," and "I want a spiritual partner." Take your time. Try to be as specific as possible. Let the thought "What I need for peace of mind" settle in your mind and the specific needs will flow naturally. Try to map as many thoughts as you can over five minutes.

For example, if you put "I need to be in control," add details: "in control of my body, my appetite, my dog, my temper, my finances, my kids, my smoking, my drinking" and so on. The more completely you express yourself, the more helpful it will be. Consider the following fields for completion, but feel free to put down any thoughts that come into your head:

- How you want your personality to be: friendly, detached, smart, giving, etc.
- How you need your appearance to be: elegant, attractive, informal, appropriate, etc.
- How you need your health to be.
- How you need to be in each of your various roles: as wife, worker, parent, son, friend, homemaker, partner, social organizer, political participant, sexual partner, spiritual practitioner, coach, etc.
- Outcomes for your various life problems: "I want my boss to be ...," "I want my wife to be ...," etc.
- Where you want to be a year from now: "I want to be, to get, to have, to become ..."; "I want a new job, to be married, to move to a new house," etc.
- Where you want to be five years from now: "to complete my master's degree," etc.
- What you want to accomplish in your life: to retire, to have children, to write that book, to be close to God, etc.
- How you require others to react: friends, family, fellow workers, boss, doctors, lawyers, politicians, priests and ministers, etc.
- What you expect of the world: home (value and condition), car, baseball team, weather, your country, other countries, the world situation, etc.

After you've written down your needs, wants, and desires, complete your map by looking at each item on it and quietly contemplating exactly what thoughts, sensations, or moods arise when that need is *not* fulfilled. Concentrate on your map; sense how your body reacts to each requirement. Take your time and be specific, writing down your emotional reaction close to each unmet need. Then draw an arrow from the need to the reaction of nonfulfillment. As John did on his map, which follows, include bodily sensations along with thoughts. The more that your response is personal and alive in the present moment, the more helpful mapping will be for you. Some items may be difficult; for these, just note your emotions and thoughts. These items hold the key. Some of your requirements may be so powerful that you may deny, repress, or project the emotional response that arises if the need goes unfulfilled. Don't worry if you overlook or pass up a requirement. It will certainly return to give you another opportunity to respond in the not-too-distant future!

Here is an example of how I respond when my need "Be well-prepared for a class" is not fulfilled: "Tension in face, apprehension, sense of distance from my material, thoughts of how the class may respond." When my need "I want people to be honest and straightforward" is unfulfilled, I experience "Irritation, tension in shoulders, sense of outrage, sinking feeling in stomach."

Look at John's "Peace of Mind" map. When his requirements are unfulfilled, his Identity System works in creative ways to confirm his damaged self. If John is experiencing feelings of being "Sad, discouraged" and having an "Empty sensation in my belly," he knows that his Identity System is in high gear. The same is true with his other reactions of "Scared, angry, fearful, heavy weight on my shoulders." Rather than assuming it's "just me," he now knows that it's "just my Identity System." This gives him a new set of options. Simply by shining the light of awareness on and embracing the thoughts and bodily sensations, he can return to a natural-functioning loop.

Upon completing his map, John expressed amazement at the global reach of his Identity System. He added details about the little requirements he had in his relationship with his wife, Laurie: "I need her to kiss me before we go to sleep; I need her to pay attention to me when I talk; I need her to give a definite answer; I need her to sound upbeat over the telephone." When she didn't do these things, his Identity System was activated. John smiled

I need to live in a place I love.

Sad, discouraged.
Empty sensation in my belly.

I need my finances to be secure.

Anxiety, fear, general tension in body.

I need to be healthy.

Peace of Mind

I need to accept myself
the way I am.

Scared, angry,
fearful, heavy weight
on my shoulders.

Frustrated, failure.
Knot in stomach.

I need to live close to my parents.

Guilty, unstable,
tightness in jaw.

I need to deepen my relationship
with Laurie.

I need to have a better
relationship with my kids.

Sad, depressed.
Pressure around head.

Bad parent, discouraged,
guilty, shoulder tension.

and said, "Wow! What a box my Identity System puts me in. It's unbelievable. Seeing it gives me a chance to have a real relationship." In fact, it has already happened. Mapping is bridging.

Your "Peace of Mind" map will have a similar pattern. Since most of your items on the map activate the Identity System, they are requirements. The greater the emotional response when the need is frustrated, the stronger the linkage to the damaged self. If you have little or no reaction to the frustration of a need, take a few minutes to do a bridging awareness practice like tuning in to background sounds or sensing your fingertips rubbing against the fabric of your clothing. If you are unable to hold on to the sounds or sensations for a period of time, your Identity System may be causing you to be disembodied. You are missing vital signals that can guide you through life. Come back to your body by integrating bridging awareness practices into your daily activities.

Emily, in one of my workshops, saw immediately after completing her "Peace of Mind" map that she had created very specific requirements of her relationships with her boss, her friends, and her sons.

"I *needed* my boss to appreciate me so I could feel like I was a good worker," she said. "I *needed* my friends to never let me down so I could feel like I was a good person. I *needed* my two sons to always be happy and well so I could feel like I was a good mom. These needs became my requirements. I've been nailing my true self into a coffin. It's as if my Identity System has tricked me into believing that to have my boss appreciate me is more important than my free-flowing self-appreciation. Needing my boss's approval was making hay for my fixer and depressor. If he appreciates me, "I'm wonderful!"—but his appreciation is never enough. I started to realize that even if my boys are angry with me or one of them is depressed about his friends, I am still a great mom. I don't need them to be happy to realize that. There is a new flow in my life. Life still has its ups and downs, but who I am can't be damaged by my boss, my sons, or my friends. I appreciate myself, my kids, and even my boss."

Once you have written down your response to your unmet needs, you have given yourself a lot of valuable information about the inner workings of your Identity System. You can track which thoughts and sensations have you dwelling in the Identity System's dark cave. The more you know about how your Identity System works, the more effective your everyday bridging practice will be.

How many "aha" experiences did you have while looking at your map? Like David, your transformation starts now. As John saw, mapping isn't only to prepare you to bridge in your daily life. It *is* bridging. Mapping shifts your consciousness right here and now. You don't have to stretch to get it; you already have it. All you have to do is rest your Identity System.

The "Peace of Mind" Map about Relationships

Taking John's lead, create a "Peace of Mind" map about what you require from the most important person in your life. Try to be as specific and detailed as possible. Here are some examples of the type of thoughts you might write down:

> "She should greet me with a long kiss and hug."

> "He should be patient when he explains things."

> "She shouldn't be all tired out when I come home."

> "She shouldn't be so emotional."

> "He should understand how hard it is to take care of the kids."

> "She shouldn't be critical of me."

"Mother should listen to me."

"He should put his dirty clothes in the hamper."

"He shouldn't rush things when we make love."

"She always has an excuse. Why does she always blame me?"

"She spends too much money."

"He drinks too much beer."

"He watches too much television."

"He shouldn't go out with the guys so often."

"She shouldn't take so long to get ready."

"He is always late."

By mapping out your emotional response when your expectation is unmet, you are able to immediately transform your relationship. Your Identity System has a picture of how your significant other should be. This picture purportedly aims solely to fix the damaged self, yet what it does is conform and support it. The Identity System works solely in the dark, and your light of awareness lessens its grip. Your emotional reactions are not due to how the other person acts; they are due solely to your Identity System. If you mindfully and openly do the mapping and experience the physical sensations caused by your Identity System, your relationships will change.

The other component of your relationship is your expectations of yourself. Recall that your Identity System has a picture of how you should be as well as how the world should be. Take a few minutes to create another map, this time of what you require of yourself. Here are some examples:

"I need be a good provider."

"I need to be a good sexual partner."

"I need to not make mistakes."

"I need to be frugal."

"I need to not drink too much."

"I need to be fun."

"I need to be friendly."

"I need to be happy."

"I need to be loving."

"I need to live a life with purpose."

"I need to be compassionate."

Complete your map as you did with the "Peace of Mind" map, writing down your emotional reaction when your requirements are unfulfilled. The requirements and emotional reactions may be subtler than on the map of what you expect of others, since these requirements form the core of your self-limited identity. The paradox is that these natural thoughts, which appear benign, will cause you unending misery and suffering and unhappiness when captured by the Identity System.

Ted is a successful small-business owner happily married to Megan. He came to a burnout-prevention workshop. Every area in his life was seemingly going well. His business was growing and profitable, he and Megan were in love, and there was no great area of friction. However, Ted was constantly worried, was slightly underweight and losing weight, and could not relax. He felt he couldn't fail his business, his workers, or his wife. His fixer map told the story. He was burned out.

His map of his relationship with Megan showed his high expectations of himself. When he tackled a project, it could never be good enough: the grass wasn't healthy or green enough; the cars had a slight problem; the service his business provided wasn't as good as it should be; he could be a better husband. In fact, he had a vision of specific acts that a perfect husband would perform: flowers for his wife every week, dinners out even when he was tired, going to the gym together. When he didn't meet his own expectations, his body let him know with chest tightness, neck tension, and a buzzing head.

During the mapping, Ted struggled with each item and progressively became more distressed. However, just before he finished, he suddenly relaxed. When discussing his map, Ted said he believed his physical symptoms were caused by a major physical problem that he was afraid to tell anyone about. Once he saw all his symptoms reappear during mapping, he *knew* that it was all due to his Identity System. With that awareness, his symptoms abated.

A week later, at his follow-up workshop, Megan came with Ted and reported that she "finally got Ted back." She explained that now when they are together, she experiences an openness and relaxation that she remembered from their courtship, saying he was less driven to do things *for* her but more interested in doing things *with* her.

A sign that an expectation has become an Identity System requirement is if you experience a repeated pattern of frustration with that particular need in your life. For example, if your relationships are usually disappointing, look at specific expectations of yourself and the other person. Your fixer has set you up for disappointment by demanding that things happen a certain way, and the depressor has you anxious that it won't last even if things do go well. Your openness to the possibility that this is an Identity System requirement already begins to heal your damaged self, and your self-esteem is less vulnerable to disappointments.

However, the purpose of the "Peace of Mind" map is not to determine which items are requirements or free thoughts. The purpose is to become familiar with free thoughts—such as "I want good working relationships"—that the Identity System is likely to capture. Without awareness, your fixer and depressor can confiscate that thought and cause you to suffer. With it, your free functioning naturally works to fulfill your needs in ways that are responsive and realistically related to the situation. When your Identity System rests, your true self always naturally manifests, and true peace of mind is available.

Peace of Mind as a Way of Life

As time goes on, you may find it helpful to create other "Peace of Mind" maps focusing on different areas of the fields listed earlier in this chapter. Since at any given point in time, your mind focuses on different aspects of your life, a series of maps will enable you to recognize additional potential Identity System requirements and gain insight into how your Identity System works. Whenever you experience pain, anguish, anger, inappropriate actions, or physical tension, it is a good time to gently entertain the possibility that an Identity System requirement is playing a part in the drama. You can do this in the heat of the moment by coming back to sensations and background sounds. This grounding in the present moment allows your awareness to expand, reducing the adverse effects of the Identity System. Being grounded in your body and surroundings, you experience a more spacious self, one that is less apt to be disturbed because it has more room in it for feelings of all kinds. With this awareness, a free thought cannot become a requirement.

Grounding yourself in the present moment allows you to see how the free thought, "My child is sick," for example, can lead to another thought, "I don't want her to be sick." This latter thought, if captured by the Identity System, generates the depressor thought that you are not a good parent. Without the light of awareness, the Identity System confiscates that thought and excites fear and bodily tension. The depressor then generates more negative thoughts about your inadequacy. The fixer grabs the opportunity to insist on immediate results, and this creates a sense of helplessness. Soon an entire storyline is generated. All of this confirms the damaged self. Left alone as a free thought, "My child is sick" stimulates a whole host of productive and free-functioning actions: you read to her, you cook her favorite soup, you slow your life down to attend to her need. You are a wonderful parent, and you are acting as one.

Just remember that peace of mind is surprisingly easy to obtain. I have spent decades analyzing the opposite of peace of mind: *fear*. Fear is born when you worry you will be unloved or abandoned or that your world will fall apart. Other causes for fear and unrest are that you will not be able to cope and that you will be injured or incapacitated. As an analyst, I have found that once people's fears are uncovered, they can deal with them. But even then the telltale signs of the Identity System remain. Since discovering the Identity System, I now know that we can do better. All of us. Fear is a free function, like shame, guilt, or doubt. It has enabled humanity to recognize danger and to protect itself. The problem with fear comes when the Identity System interferes with this natural function. It may detract from it, causing you to not address a situation, or it may amplify it, either overwhelming you into a paralysis of inaction or overstimulating you to over-reaction.

By resting your Identity System, fear and physical tension will not trample over you. To find peace, you do not need to analyze the source of your fear or try to overcome it. The need to understand it is simply Identity System–driven. Bridging and mapping require nothing more of you than to be aware of and thereby rest your Identity System. Peace will flow from there.

9
Turn Off Channel Me and Live Your Best Life

Channel Me offers two choices for your viewing pleasure. The first is produced and directed by your depressor. The depressor takes everyday events and uses them to create high dramas of misery and suffering. Now turn the channel to fixer productions. The fixer offers higher levels of endorphins and an escape from the mundane events of your life. It also specializes in high drama, featuring your own dreams, hopes, and ambitions.

Behind the scenes of these dueling dramas are your storylines. Your mind stores and processes information with thoughts; it then organizes, reviews, and acts on these thoughts with storylines. Here's an example: I say "jump," and before you can jump, you need a story to illustrate what jumping looks like. Before humans can act in any way, we need a story to create a mental picture of that action. Stories enable babies to sit, crawl, walk, and talk. Stories accompany most of your daily activities. Athletes use them to envision their trip down the ski slope, through the pool, or along the balance beam.

Stories are simply natural functioning—they allow you to live your best life.

But like the best of natural thoughts, your stories can be captured by the Identity System. The key is to recognize when this happens. To do this, all you have to do is observe when your storylines and dramas take you away from the present moment. When they do, you want to arrest your Identity System before it collapses your awareness, disconnects you from your senses, and impairs your natural functioning. Simply recognizing when Channel Me comes on is enough to bring you back to your full life.

Catching the flu, losing a credit card, missing a plane, being rejected by a friend, having car trouble, making mistakes, losing money on the stock market, going to the dentist, and locking oneself out of one's apartment—no big deal, right? That's right— when it happens to someone else. But if one of these everyday setbacks happens to you, your Identity System may run with it, creating a high drama of suffering: Channel Me is on the air. Once your Identity System runs with depressor themes, you'll quickly observe the signs of an active Identity System, including such self-defeating thoughts as "Why did I do this? I should have known better. Why is it always me?" Don't let your Identity System convince you that Channel Me is your only option. It does not accurately depict who you are, no matter how vivid and clear the picture. The longer you tune in to Channel Me, the more you reinforce the damaged self.

Your Fixer Channel Is Not Playing a Reality Show

The fixer theme of Channel Me is upbeat and pleasant, helping you escape your life as you plan for a better future. This makes it a bit more challenging to deal with. Who wouldn't want to tune in to a channel where life is better, you are successful, and your aspirations are totally fulfilled? But consider whether the fixer can ever bring peace of mind.

The fixer is often disguised when you are thinking about an unresolved issue. For example, a friend has backed out on you again; instead of dealing with your disappointment and anger honestly at the time, you said nothing. Now, hours later, as you try to sleep, you know clearly what actions needed to have been taken. You replay them numerous times, alternating between anger and self-critical talk. You are too tense to sleep well because your Identity System has you in full gear, "fixing your problem." The fix is illusory because in reality, your Identity System is bolstering your damaged self. The only solution, and it is an easy one, is to switch on your light of awareness, shine it on your Identity System, and use an awareness practice to go to sleep.

Sure, the fixer can weave beautiful stories to help you escape from experiencing life's unpleasantries. Tuning in to Channel Me allows you to tune out some of the pain of the depressor, but it also tunes you away from your life itself. Here's an example: You are home alone, caught in the depressor channel. It's unpleasant, so you switch to the fixer channel. It is ready, as always, with stories of a better life: "If only I were to do this, then my life would be much easier, happier, and less stressful." You name the problem, and the fixer can conjure up a remedy. Your endorphins flow as your perfect life plays out in your head. But each second you tune in to Channel Me is a second lost from your life, keeping you from the only place you can live: the right here and right now. You are worshipping the Identity System while it is stealing your life away.

Your dreams, hopes, and ambitions make good drama for Channel Me. The following class discussion shows how the participants learned to defuse their storylines.

Monique: "You really dropped a bomb when you wanted us to use our dreams, hopes, and ambitions in the 'Peace of Mind' map. I was moving right along, but now I am experiencing a lot of fear about losing my dreams."

Stan: "Mapping simply allows you to see how your Identity System interferes with the fruition of your natural, free-functioning dreams, hopes, and ambitions."

Monique: "I guess my fear is my damaged self, isn't it?"

David: "I was as worried about losing my dreams as Monique, but when I look at my ambitions, it's true, I never found the pot of gold at the end of the rainbow. When I was a child, I dreamed of being a baseball player, a pitcher. I worked hard and made the high school baseball team. I pitched and won a lot of games, but I was never satisfied. There was always someone better. After I realized that I wasn't going to make it to the Major Leagues, I dreamed of going to a good college, and I was admitted to an Ivy League school. Next, after graduation, I dreamed of getting a good job. I ended up being paid more than I had ever imagined. None of these accomplishments gave me peace of mind. Now I'm anxious about holding on to the job. Good reviews didn't give me a sense of well-being. Impending disaster was always just around the corner."

Monique: "Yes, it's the same for me. Marrying the man of my dreams didn't settle my mind. Having the most magnificent, healthy, and beautiful baby was wonderful, but it didn't settle my mind, either. In fact, after my dreams were fulfilled, I always became sad, feeling empty."

Stan: "These are examples of how the Identity System takes free thoughts—be a high school pitching star, graduate at the top of your college class, get a good job, marry a good man, have a perfect baby—and hooks them into the damaged self. When your ambitions are apparently fulfilled, your restless, damaged self is still not healed. Your fixer develops another goal, hoping this will make you feel whole and complete. Your depressor creates frustration and depression, which actualizes the damage. Finally, either your depressor makes you feel like a failure or your fixer blames it on others or the world. Either way, the damage is perpetuated. All this supplies storylines for Channel Me."

David: "Being aware of my hopes and ambitions and how they are tied up with my Identity System is painful yet gives me a freedom I have never known."

Monique: "I'm beginning to see how a dream, hope, or ambition can start out as free functioning. I think, for instance, 'Have a baby.' If the Identity System enlists this thought, it becomes a pawn for the Identity System to use. It isn't a free thought anymore. There's an impossible regimen of requirements, and I don't get to freely enjoy my baby just as she is. Don't get me wrong—having and caring for my little one is a wonderful experience, and I wouldn't give it up for anything; all the same, guilt over not being a good-enough mother and worry were often around. Now I understand they are fixer and depressor add-ons."

Stan: "You are discovering that the Identity System is the one and only thing that interferes with your natural free functioning. Wanting to have a baby and enjoying and caring for her are natural free functions when you respond to things as they are rather than to your Identity System's requirements. Those natural free functions are expressions of your true self, actualizations of your Source. It is a holy and glorious activity."

Letting Your Identity System
Be Your Guide

Your Identity System is a blessing. It really is. Every time you see it, it shows you the way to your true self and to natural functioning. For example, let's say your house needs cleaning. You look around, see the dust and dirt, and have a free thought, "I have the time, and I'll do some housework." Soon, the Identity System kicks in: "It's too nice a day to do housework. Why don't I have help? Who cares if the house is messy or dirty? It's none of their business anyway! This is not what I went to college for!" If you do not recognize the Identity System's activity, you become full of tension, irritability, and resentment, or you try to escape from being present in the moment with pleasant daydreams. By the act of being aware that this is the activity of your Identity System, you have given yourself the opportunity of returning to the present moment—sights, sounds, bodily sensations, and thoughts—and resuming your free functioning.

Simply sweeping, dusting, vacuuming, and scrubbing with a ready, relaxed mind is free functioning. If irritable or resentful thoughts come to mind, give them space—labeling helps—and return to cleaning. When you are freely functioning in the moment, you naturally integrate your Source while healing the damaged self. As you continue, the natural, non-dualistic true self emerges, freely functioning as doing housework. The "problem" of housework is not the activity itself but how the Identity System taints it with negative thoughts and bodily sensations.

Mapping is a very active process to bring insight into your life. The maps you've created can work for you by letting your Identity System point you toward your true self and helping you regain your full vitality and integrity. As time goes by, you may create some personalized maps that might be helpful for you. For now, let's take a tour of some more useful maps.

The Project Map

Use the Project map when you are planning a project of some significance, like buying a new car or a house. Mind-body mapping projects help you see how the Identity System creates resistance that interferes with free functioning. The Project map lessens the Identity System's impact, but it doesn't outline how you should proceed or guarantee you a successful outcome. It simply spotlights your resistance so you can then bridge and carry on with free functioning.

To create a Project map, write down the project—such as "Buying a house"—in the center of a blank piece of paper and take four or five minutes to jot down your associations. Then look for Identity System involvement such as fixer or depressor activities, emotionally charged items, or Identity System repetitive themes. Once you identify your Identity System interference, you have the green light to function freely.

The Nemesis Map

For the Nemesis map, take five minutes to map your reaction to a person or situation that is repeatedly menacing to you, such as going to the dentist or visiting a troubling relative. Sometimes we are our own nemesis. You can map this as well. The "Favorite Daily Drama" map is a similar map; on it, you start with the personal storyline that your Identity System uses to take you away from being present in the moment. Your personal drama, such as "Poor little me, if only I had this or didn't have that, none of this would be bugging me," only embellishes the false sense of who you are. Mapping these storylines helps you recognize them, allowing you to turn off Channel Me.

The Pain Map

Create a Pain map when you're feeling despair due to pain—mental or physical. Pain is a part of the human experience. It is important to understand that pain is a combination of sensations and thoughts. The thought "I am in pain" is a concept that the Identity System may use to limit awareness, constricting your life around your pain and your efforts to control it. Of course, pain is real, and when it manifests, you should not ignore it. Unlike labeling a thought, it is not helpful to label your physical sensations. The key is to acknowledge the painful sensation and to broaden your awareness so that it becomes only a small part of your total picture. When you have a tunnel vision of pain, the resilience and natural healing of the body is impaired. When the Identity System is active, fear and tension intensify pain's physical and mental components. Pain in turn supports the Identity System's mission of sustaining the damaged self. As time goes on, more and more requirements become interwoven with the pain-thoughts and painful sensations. All of that interferes with natural healing and with free functioning.

Labeling and mapping allow you to expand your awareness to see the part the Identity System is playing in your experience of pain. Expanded awareness and a resting Identity System optimize the natural healing process. You don't create a Pain map to "fix" pain; you map to bridge your Identity System, which lets you naturally move to a freer, more relaxed and resilient state. As described in chapter 3, in my workshops for sufferers of chronic pain, participants note that when they are present in the moment, the quality of the pain starts to change and even move around. Sufferers become less constricted and defined by their condition.

Your Dreams Are a Playground for Your Identity System

Dreaming is a natural organizing and processing function, and it's as vital to your well-being as all the other functions of your body. Its purpose is to heal and to create physical, mental, and spiritual health. When open loops are not processed during the day, they continue to be automatically processed at night in your dreams, whether or not they were caused by events or by your Identity System. When the deep sleep needed for dreams is continuously interrupted, the brain becomes dysfunctional.

The hardware for dreams is supplied by your biological system. The software, or content, is primarily supplied by the Identity System. Freud, in *The Interpretation of Dreams*, postulated that wish fulfillment drives a person's dreams. Identity System theory postulates that the Identity System's core belief of being damaged and incomplete drives and supplies the software for dreams. If you recall your dreams, each one is an attempt to either fix or reinforce the damaged self. Dreams of not being able to escape harm or of being embarrassed, weak, helpless, or inadequate express and reinforce the damaged self. Dreams of winning or of being successful, admired, or heroic are attempts to fix the damaged self. Win, lose, or draw, it is all Identity System, whether they are depressor or fixer dreams. If you doubt that you have a core belief of being damaged, just transcribe your dreams as soon as you awaken for a couple of weeks.

In addition to the dream images, the feeling tone of the dream is important. Fearful states, excited states, "blah" states, and happy states are as important as the storyline. Freud also noted that opposites can have the same meaning: one person, thought, or image can symbolically represent another; many thoughts can be condensed onto one; and daytime associations are related to dream thoughts and images. He believed that dreams were the royal road to the unconscious and, when interpreted correctly, could unlock neurotic symptoms.

With a strong Identity System, dreams fill your body-mind with anxiety, visceral helplessness, and bodily tension. As the Identity System rests with bridging, the repetitive quality of certain dreams decreases and you awaken more refreshed. Dreaming resumes its natural function of processing open loops and creating wellness instead of reinforcing or fixing the damaged self. Dream mapping is indeed a royal road to seeing the Identity System's functioning.

The Dream Map

To create a Dream map, put a specific dream theme, content, or image you have encountered repeatedly in the center circle—such as being chased, being hurt, winning, or being a hero—and put dream thoughts and current thoughts anywhere on the paper. Add sensations you feel now or felt in the dream. If you awaken with strong emotions but with vague dream content, just place the feelings generated by the dream in the center circle—helplessness, suffering, happiness—and add the associated sensations and thoughts. Don't spend over five minutes on any Dream map. Don't analyze the map. Just let it help you expand your awareness of the nature and functioning of your Identity System. The true meaning of dreams can never be grasped by words or images. With Dream mapping, as with all Identity System principles and practices, the focus is on seeing the resistance. You can map your Identity System. You cannot map truth.

Take a look at Sam's Dream map, which follows. He labeled it with a specific dream about his wife: "Theresa Rejects Me." We went over his map in a workshop and had the following discussion:

Stan: "How did the dream make you feel?"

Sam: "I felt beat up . . . exhausted, as if I'd just come out of a washing machine. Usually I wake refreshed, but this morning I was a loser. I also felt disappointed in Theresa. That's what was so crazy—I knew it was only a dream—but I felt angry with her. The day before the dream, I was disappointed because she seemed far away. I didn't complain; that wouldn't have done any good. She loves me, but she can be moody."

Sam's "Theresa Rejects Me" Dream Map

She has no time for me.

The building in the dream
was big. I was little and old.

Theresa has been so busy
at work. Then she has to
drive Tyler to basketball practice.

Theresa shut me out
in the cold.

In the dream I was
nearly dead.

It was like I might die before
I got home.

Why won't Theresa help?

Theresa Rejects Me

I don't like being sick.

I woke feeling a hangover
from the dream.

I'm really independent, but in
the dream I was really sick.

Can't do without her.

Being passive.

Won't be able to help myself.

Being a loser.

Being weak.

149

Stan: "What did you learn about your Identity System from this map, Sam?"

Sam: "That's easy—it's all Identity System! My depressor was in charge. The dream presents me as little, helpless, rejected, cold, weak, sick, dependent, and needy! I'd say that's 'damaged.' It's pure damaged-self stuff. I don't see much fixer."

Stan: "Could you be looking to Theresa to fix your damage?"

Sam: "But she can't fix the damage."

Stan: "All Identity Systems look for impossible fixes."

Sam: "I see. If I experience the sense of damage and then look to the fixer to heal it, that is only pouring salt on the wound. Throughout the day, I remember, whenever I had weak, helpless feelings, my fixer would jump in: 'Work harder! Fight! Don't give in!' I did that fixer stuff all day, and still the sense of damage remained. You told us once, 'The fixer cannot heal the damaged self.'"

Stan: "Let's see how that understanding can help you with your Dream map and also in your daily life. What else do you see about your map?"

Sam: "Well, first, I see that I've been secretly blaming Theresa. I accept now that she can't fix me. I wanted her to because I felt incomplete and weak. That old pattern can only spoil our relationship. Just knowing I was looking to her for a fix and knowing that she can't fix me makes me feel better, less tensed up. Now I have some space to see how it is for her. It's funny. When we got married, she had many strong traits that seemed to balance my weak traits. My fixer led me to want more from Theresa than she could possibly give. It had me denying my weak traits. It was like pushing a spring down. It pops back with a vengeance. I am thinking now that maybe I don't need to push away the helpless feelings. All of a sudden, I feel closer to Theresa. I don't need to resent her for not fixing me. My fixer had me fearing that those 'little baby' feelings would make me a helpless little boy."

Stan: "Expanding your awareness shifts you out of a self-centered state where you are the victim. When you expanded your awareness to embrace your depressor, your appreciation of Theresa expanded. By bridging your Identity System, you transcended that old dualistic world. Your awareness of yourself and of Theresa does not have to be limited to any dualistic concepts such as good/bad, weak/strong, or dependent/independent."

Sam: "I am already feeling a lot more freedom in my life. I'm going to be more attentive to my thoughts and to the knot in my stomach when my fixer and depressor get going. But I have a question: How would you work with a positive dream? For instance, a few days ago I dreamed I was playing basketball. It was a close game. I leaped high and dunked the ball. My hands were big, or rather, the ball was small, so I had a lot of control."

Stan: "Let's look at a dream with a positive flavor. What was your feeling when you awoke?"

Sam: "I felt great! I woke refreshed and full of energy. It would be great to have those feelings every day. There is a puzzle here. The dream gave me a good start to the day, but from the work we've just done, I'm questioning how the fixer can give me a good deal."

Stan: "Why don't you do a quick Dream map and see if we can answer your question?" (A few minutes pass as Sam writes up a map he calls the Basketball Dream map.)

Sam's Basketball Dream Map

Having big hands.

Being in control.

Being a winner.

Father had big hands.

Getting respect.

Basketball

Dream

Hearing cheers.

Feeling great.

Dunking ball.

Being graceful.

Being energetic.

Being competitive.

Easy.

Sam: "When I look at this map, all the items seem positive: 'Being a winner,' 'Being in control,' 'Getting respect,' 'Being competitive,' 'Being energetic,' 'Feeling great.' The Basketball Dream map is nearly the opposite of the 'Theresa Rejects Me' Dream map. The Theresa dream was obviously full of damage, like 'Being a loser,' 'Being passive,' 'Being weak,' and so on. I'm now thinking that most of these positive items in the basketball dream are not free thoughts but rather are fixer requirements."

Stan: "That may be true, and it's always important to consider that possibility. If these thoughts are fixer requirements, there will always be a depressor hiding underneath."

Sam: "Well, the point is that later in the day after the basketball dream, which seemed so positive, I had a meeting with my boss. The meeting went well, but still I came out of it, as usual, feeling down."

Stan: "The Identity System always lets you down because it is the fixer who pushes you up. The higher you reach, the harder you fall. Either way, all you have to do is wake up, come to your senses, and be aware."

Sam: "That's the true self. That is being one with the Source."

Sam's two Dream maps appeared to be so different, yet in both, he relied on his Identity System for his sense of self. In the Theresa dream, he bought into his depressor, and in the basketball dream, he identified with his fixer. Both confirmed his damaged self and masked his true self. Whenever you restrict yourself to an identity, good or bad, you confine yourself to a box that holds unhappiness. Your true self is dynamic, ever changing, and not confined. It is vast, inconceivable, and all-embracing. It is with you right here, right now.

Turning off Channel Me during the day is as easy as turning off a light. By simply being cognizant of your Identity System, you can live your life at its best. At night, your Identity System gives you the opportunity to recognize its dysfunctional open loops as presented in your dreams. Dream mapping allows you to restore and strengthen your physical, mental, and spiritual balance. When Channel Me no longer dominates your days, your nights become the havens of rest they should be.

10

Your Search for Value in Your Existence

Universally, humans yearn to live life well and to be in connection with the Source of all life. The world's religions testify to this search for existential value, asking such questions as "How did we get here?" "Where are we going?" "What is our life?" and "How should we live our life?" Religions direct our lives toward the living word of God. In the Bible, the Torah, the Vedas, and the Koran, the "Word" is God's law, and God's word and man's behavior are inseparable.

From time immemorial, the barrier to finding this unity with God—or the purpose of life—is, of course, the Identity System. Its whole premise, as you saw in chapter 1, is limitation and restriction. Bridging and mapping, by resting your Identity System, help you answer your questions about your life's purpose and meaning. They lift you out of the limiting fog of your own Identity System and take you into real life so you can function freely in a unified world of harmonious differences. Bridging allows you to know that you are never separate from the Source at any moment. No matter how powerful your false self is, bridging creates a unity in the right here, right now.

Your Relative Value versus Absolute Value

Relative values are found throughout all civilizations. Money is the prime example of how society places differing values on people, products, services, and even ideas. A corporate CEO may be valued by his board of directors at $500,000 per year, while a production worker in the same company may be assigned an annual value of $35,000. The Identity System loves this kind of valuing, which creates separation and assigns relative values to your work, your goals, and even to yourself. However, this Identity System–driven system of values does not acknowledge your own absolute value—a value that cannot be measured, quantified, or compared to others. Your Identity System does not integrate and can never allow you to function freely and in unity with all of creation. It will never allow you to do God's will.

Bridging brings you back to your own natural functioning, which allows you to integrate the relative and absolute value of your activities and, hence, of yourself. Your relative value as a professional athlete, for example, may be dramatically reduced by injury; as a corporate executive, your value would be reduced by a debilitating stroke. But the absolute value of your true self is never reduced. The Identity System, however, automatically negates your own absolute value whenever you negate the absolute value of your present activity. When you fail to appreciate both the absolute and relative value of sweeping the floor, you manifest and confirm the damaged self. When you appreciate the absolute value of the activity, you actualize your own absolute value. For example, cleaning the house does not decrease the value of your true self any more than playing with the children increases it. When you're functioning naturally and freely, you clean the house when it needs it, and you play with the children when the time is right. Rest your Identity System, and you'll know when the time is right.

Once the Identity System creates separation and relativity, the absolute value of a person, idea, or thing automatically disappears. All that is left is a materialistic world. Absolute value does not mean that differences do not exist. It is natural to choose a shiny apple rather than a shriveled one. Nevertheless, be aware that the rotten apple is a perfect manifestation of a rotten apple. It may be food for other creatures, or it may decay into soil-enriching compost. When you can appreciate the absolute and relative value of both apples, your awareness expands from the polarized, tension-filled Identity System world of good versus bad apples to a unified world of harmonious differences. Appreciating both the relative and absolute value of both kinds of apples, you are free to select appropriately. In another example, even if a person is convicted of stealing, his absolute value is not lessened any more than a child's innate goodness is diminished by his fibs. However, the criminal's absolute value does not negate the natural law of cause and effect or the religious/judicial codes of morality and justice. This appreciation of both absolute and relative value and making appropriate choices is the essence of free functioning.

To experience this harmony and balance with the Source, you need a resting Identity System. By practicing mapping and bridging, you come back to your senses and expand your awareness, appreciating differences and making informed choices. If you choose to sweep the floor, you can then appreciate the chore without any overlays of guilt, depression, or anxiety that you are wasting your time. You can quietly give thanks to the dirt on the floor, the broom, your hands that hold the broom, and your mind that directs the activity. If you choose to take a walk instead, you appreciate the sun on your face, the gentle breeze, and the movement of your body.

The issue of absolute value leads to God. In the next example, Jeff, by resting his overactive Identity System, became ready to explore the deeper aspects of his spirituality.

Jeff was a successful financial planner, and he felt pride in always having answers for his clients. He left no variable unaddressed. For himself and his clients, he crafted detailed plans on how to reach financial critical mass by retirement—having enough accumulated capital to live off of interest and dividends. During a workshop, Jeff began to see that his fixer's need to be in control of his future and his clients' futures, while contributing to his monetary success, was causing havoc in his personal life. He couldn't leave work issues or behavior at the office. He could never let others manage a situation, and his wife resented his intrusions into her sphere of influence. He was not able to let his children solve their own problems, and he was often jumping in and "fixing" their small issues and quandaries for them.

After two weeks of bridging classes, Jeff found he had become adept at resting his Identity System. Life became a more peaceful and relaxed journey for him. At the last session he said that he had one remaining area he wanted to clarify: his relationship to God. The rest of the class was amenable to creating their own maps about religion and spirituality. Each person chose their own subject, such as these:

> "Is there a God?"

> "Do I need religion?"

> "What is life after death?"

> "Can good Christians be self-centered?"

> "At times, I feel I don't need religion."

> "Giving is hard for me."

The Spirituality Map

If you have similar questions about religion or spirituality, try to map one of your questions or concerns. Mapping doesn't show you which spiritual path to take. Instead, it reveals what is interfering with your ability to pursue your own path. Bridging and mapping simply remove specific hindrances to living a natural, full life.

Write your question in the center of a piece of paper. Circle it, and work quickly and loosely to scatter your thoughts around the paper. When you're done, look at Jeff's "Does God Exist?" map, which follows. It is full of questions about purpose, values, and beginning and ending, all of which are natural questions of a free-functioning mind.

Jeff chose his thought, "What happens when I die?" as the first item on his map. As he talked about this statement, he described feeling pending disaster and panic. He talked of imagining being dead and said that his skin was starting to crawl. He immediately noted that his Identity System was in action, exploiting uncertainty with the requirement "I need answers." When concrete answers are not forthcoming, the body reacts as Jeff's did: with physical tension, fear, and worry. The question did not trigger his fear; his Identity System did.

"My damaged self is in the driver's seat," he noted, and then he smiled, aware now that he knew what to do to rest his Identity System: "I can only act in the moment. Hearing the fan noise, feeling the texture of my shirt and the pressure on my butt, and sitting and talking. My awareness opens. My doubts about death fade, and I'm alive and kicking. Pushing away the painful stuff gives my depressor something to ruminate about. The central question "Does God exist" is open. I don't need an answer here and now; all I have to do is live my life with caring and compassion."

Your mind, functioning freely, with and without doubt, and naturally, with and without questions, will move you toward your

Is God like a person—
or some universal field?

Why do bad things
happen to good people?

I don't give it any consideration
during my everyday life.

Is God the creator of everything?

What if the answer is "No!"?

Does

God Exist?

He must!
How did I get here?

What is the purpose?

What is my relationship to God?

What happens when I die?

This is a bigger problem
than I thought.

Like some ocean of energy.

What is the base of all my values?

spiritual center. The pursuit of certainty may be your Identity System busy at work. When you grasp for the ungraspable, you can only experience limitation and a sense of damage. The Identity System search for certainty does not enable or empower you to fully and freely live. Bridge, and your damaged self transforms into the expansive true self. With that expansive vision, your problems, questions, and answers dissolve in God's hands.

Living as we do in an era of ever-expanding scientific achievements, we have all come to expect that every question will have an answer, and every problem a solution. All it takes for those answers and solutions, we feel, is sufficient scientific study. For example, we expect a cure for cancer at some point. Nevertheless, while science and logic are great gifts, they become a problem when they become our masters instead of our servants.

A classmate of Jeff's, who had the same central question about God's existence, commented, "I exist. God exists. Jesus exists. Whenever my Identity System is active, I doubt. When it's resting, I know. The scriptures are the truth, and when my Identity System is resting, I not only know but act accordingly."

Another classmate added, "When my Identity System rests, I pray for the whole world; when it is active, I pray for myself." How true! Compassion, bonding, and acts of loving-kindness flow freely with a resting Identity System.

Bridging leads you to clarity of your spiritual base at each moment. While your clarity may fluctuate, your spiritual center does not. Bridging the Identity System can help enhance your sense of clarity, as this story shows:

Lucy is quite religious. She talked nostalgically about how close she had felt to God the preceding summer when she had attended a church camp. Now she felt far from God, and she was ready to quit college because of finances. She had had to reduce her course load so she could work enough to pay the bills. She was depressed about having to work two jobs—as a waitress in a restaurant and as a housecleaner. I asked her if she was any further from God when she was scrubbing toilets than when she was at church camp, and she broke out in a big smile, laughed, and relaxed. She was then able to see how she had requirements: that she would not need to clean toilets or work in a restaurant. If those requirements were unmet, Lucy experienced herself as damaged, and in her mind damaged meant separation from the Almighty. She came to see that the only thing separating her from God is her Identity System. To experience wholeness, completeness, and in her words, "the presence of the Holy Father," all she needs to do is rest her Identity System, no matter where she is—in a bathroom stall or praying in a chapel.

Living by a religious tradition or not, all of us wrestle with the divine mystery. As you lead your life right now, you are continuing the tradition of the human dialogue with the Source. Each of us is challenged to bridge our personal Identity System and return to our true self. Each can become a vital link in the ongoing human tradition. Bridging is a universal method, allowing all of us to experience and express the Source in everyday life. As you unify your behavior with the Source, your character naturally purifies. Your life and the life of the universe move toward harmony and balance.

The key is what you do with your life. It is not a matter of believing or not believing, as these are merely thoughts that cannot limit the reality of your vast, unfathomable relationship with your Source. The question of whether God exists is important to explore, and it can be mapped to help you understand the underlying "baggage" we bring to the religious table.

11

By Embracing Death, You Experience Life

Influenced by the youth-oriented culture we live in, our Identity Systems have us worshipping an idealized vision of youth, beauty, wellness, and life. Since unending youth and beauty are unattainable, and sickness and death are inevitable, we're led down a dead-end path to the damaged self. Only by embracing sickness, old age, and death can you be liberated from your Identity System and resume your Source-fed life.

It is time to fully realize the consequences of bondage to individual and collective Identity Systems: extreme anxiety and fear generated by the thought of death. Let's look at death from the standpoint of bridging. Natural life—the harmonious world of differences—contains all opposites, including birth and death, even at the cellular level. In 2002, biologists Sydney Brenner, John E. Sulston, and H. Robert Horvitz won the Nobel Prize for their work exploring "death genes," genes that are programmed to end the life of a cell. They hypothesize that when the death gene shuts down, overgrowth of cells occurs, which may lead to cancer. If the death gene is hyperactive, cells may die off prematurely in diseases such as AIDS and Alzheimer's. The life-giving gene and the death-giving gene create the balanced system of life. Life is inseparable from death. For many of us, the idea that our own genes contain programs for death, even before birth, is uncomfortable. It seems easier to accept an idea of cells simply wearing out rather than having a built-in program that dooms us from conception. Sigmund Freud faced a similar reaction when he was criticized for postulating the "death drive," or death instinct, to account for self-induced suffering in human beings. Many psychoanalysts preferred the concept of the aggressive drive rather than the death drive.

This discovery of the death program present at birth can help to break down our reluctance to accept death. Without death, life could not exist. Each moment, death is essential to growth, renewal, nourishment, and all the natural processes, including health. Rejecting death only creates a stronger separation of the self, and this fuels the Identity System's damaged self. Rejecting death, sickness, and unhappiness only strengthens the damaged self; denying hardship causes hardship. Many who suffer deepen their suffering because of the depressor-driven thought that God has abandoned them. But the Source of all embraces life and death. As the Nobel laureates found, the body clearly uses both the life and the death program to function. The Identity System also uses the life and death program in fulfilling its mission of separation. For example, the depressor is an analog of the death program. It functions solely to express damage. In the extreme case of suicide, the death program reigns as the Identity System kills off the biological system. On the other hand, the Identity System's persistence in maintaining the separation of the self and a perpetual-motion fixer demonstrates an uncontrollable life program. Here the Identity System is not naturally limiting its own growth. It grows uncontrollably, not unlike cancer cells, and causes suffering and even death of the body-mind by sickness or suicide.

The Death Map

Trace the workings of your Identity System regarding death. Again, draw a small circle in the center of a blank sheet of paper and write "Death" in the circle. Freely allow your thoughts to arise, and then scatter them on the paper.

Look at Carla's Death map, which follows, with its great variety of ideas. After creating her map, her conception of death expanded, bringing her peace and a feeling of inclusiveness, as this conversation shows:

Carla: "Well, you've taught us to look for the depressor or the fixer. First, it was painful to do this, but as I went deeper, I became more intimate with my sadness, and my mind became quieter. That's when I heard the birds chirping outside the window and the cars going by. It was as if my body relaxed into the sadness. The sad thoughts lessened. Then my depressor hit me with thoughts of rotting in the ground, Ellie's eventual death, the death of my cat, Uncle Louie's death, my brother Frank killing himself day by day with his addiction, my emptiness. Looking now at the map, I see it's obvious how my Identity System uses all these thoughts to reinforce the damaged self. My Identity System has all these morbid storylines about death to confirm my separation, incompleteness, and imperfections. I hate to see Ellie sick. Last winter, when she had a middle ear infection and a ruptured eardrum, I became fearful that the infection would go to her brain. It seemed so close to her brain. It was a bad experience

Carla's Death Map

Body exhausted.

Stomachache.

Emptiness.

Listening to sounds.

Go to heaven.

What will they do with my body?

My brother is killing himself.

Rotting in the ground.

Bird song.

Death

Cat's death.

What is heaven?

Uncle Louie died;
I couldn't look at him in the casket.

What's God?

Free up soul from body.

Morbid.

Judgment.

What will happen to my daughter?

Fear.

Terror.

Makes me feel like throwing up.

I must be first; I can't stand the thought of my daughter's death.

for me. But she did get better, and soon enough she was well again."

Stan: "Carla, tell me, who dies when you take your final breath?"

Carla: "It's me."

Stan: "Is it? Is it really you, or is it your Identity System's conception of you?"

Carla: "That's hard. Of course, it is my Identity System's conception of who I think I am, but this body right here dies, doesn't it?"

Stan: "Certainly, the body dies—but is that body all there is to your true self? Does your true self die when your body dies?"

Carla: "When I'm thinking like this, I'd answer yes, but when my Identity System is quiet, then I think no—I am expansive. I include more than just this."

Stan: "How expansive?"

Carla: "When I am really quiet and aware, or during mass, my true self is very big, very inclusive. It embraces, well, really everyone, everything."

Stan: "Can it be damaged? Can it end or have a limit?"

Carla: "No. It is limitless."

Stan: "So your true self cannot be damaged even by death?"

Carla: "Death still feels very bad, but no, my true self can't be damaged. It even embraces death."

Stan: "So does your true self go beyond your conceptions and imaginations of death—and of life and death?"

Carla: "Yes. So when this heart stops for good, my Identity System's conception of the little separate 'I' dies, but my true self embraces everything—all life and death. It excludes nothing. It embraces all my fearful thoughts and my dread of death, even the thoughts of Ellie's death. My faith, strengthened by bridging, gives me peace."

Expanding Your Boundaries beyond Death

Carla's question about the end of life goes beyond the realm of the intellect, beyond the realm of the Identity System. In order to gain some insight into death's effect on the true self, let us turn to an experiential exercise based on the work of Dennis Genpo Merzel, author of *The Path of the Human Being* and *The Eye Never Sleeps*. This exercise is helpful not only in enabling you to experience an expanded state of consciousness (awareness) but in allowing you to see your Identity System's attempt to constrict your awareness. Let your Identity System rest by doing some bridging exercises. Listen to the noises around you—a cat purring, a distant television, a fan running in a bathroom. Sense the smoothness of this book's cover. Label any thoughts that arise. Now relax in a chair in a quiet room, close your eyes, and look into your mind to see if you find any limits to your consciousness. Take your time and slowly consider whether there are any limits to your expansiveness to your left, to your right, forward, backward, up, and down. Quietly and gently, search for your boundaries. Continue your search for several minutes. Look hard and deep inside.

When you finish, take your time to look within and ask yourself, "How big is my expanded state of consciousness. How big is my mind?" Try to experience the answer with a resting Identity System rather than by trying to figure it out. There are no right or wrong answers. Frequently come back to your body's sensations and to background sounds. If you're like many of my workshop participants, the answer to "How big is my mind?" is "Very big." Just be aware that even in an exercise designed to rest it, the Identity System can make you feel like a failure. So if you didn't experience the peace and tranquillity of an expanded state, no matter. The boundless treasury of your true self is with you each moment, regardless of any exercise. Just become aware that your Identity System is preventing you from experiencing that fact.

People have strong reactions to this exercise. In a workshop, when I asked, "What are your boundaries?" Rosa at first began to relax and feel her boundaries fall away, but then she tensed and became frightened as she felt like a dark wall began to close her in. That wall was her Identity System, containing her within a narrow vision of herself and preventing her from entering a state of expanded consciousness.

When I asked, "When will you die?" Larry lost the feelings of spaciousness and felt his Identity System physically attacking him, tensing his shoulders and constricting his head. As he described this, he began to smile, however, realizing for the first time that despite its effect on him, the word *die* is only a word that he was allowing to put his whole being into a tailspin.

David described feeling peaceful, expansive, endless, and just plain big, until a thought occurred: "How can I, David, be endless?" His depressor had succeeded in making him feel, as he described it, separate and limited, out of touch with the people and sounds around him. He said he physically slumped in his chair. David recovered wonderfully, though, by bridging back to his whole self. Out of this encounter, he learned that by trying to define, explain, or analyze the true self, you can become damaged. The true self is too big to conceptualize.

The direct experience of expanded awareness embraces everything, but it is not deceived by anything. It includes all doubts and all questions and all issues—like a boundless ocean, its vast expanse includes all the passing waves.

Old age, sickness, and death are vital elements of the human condition. Your Identity System captures free thoughts that appreciate life, wellness, beauty, and youth. From them, it creates requirements for an idealized life. Failure to live that life reinforces the damaged self. By mapping old age, sickness, and death, you can see your Identity System's strategy and recognize the depressor/fixer cycles. Bridging awareness practice enables you to expand your awareness to embrace life as it is rather than the Identity System misconceptions. Life becomes an adventure.

12
Life Can Be Beautiful

Your goal in buying this book is transformation: to experience the fullness of yourself and all your possibilities. To transform is not at all an abstract notion but a very concrete and recognizable change in the way you live day to day. I hope you'll be inspired by the following examples of how bridging and mapping changed the lives of some of the workshop participants whom you've met throughout the book.

Carla

Carla spoke of how befriending her Identity System transformed how she mothered her young daughter. Parenting has become easier and more joyful.

"I'm much more alive and more attentive to my life. With my daughter, Ellie, I notice her cues quicker and respond earlier. In the evenings, I sense when she's tired; I don't wait until she becomes irritable before I respond.

"I'm more aware of my own thoughts, and less carried away by them. My thoughts are becoming my helpers. They point out choices I need to be aware of. Thoughts are not bossing me around. For example, Ellie always wants big portions on her plate, especially desserts—bigger than she could possibly eat. In the past, I'd think, 'She can't possibly eat all that!' Then other thoughts would follow: 'Why should she be limited as I was when I was growing up?' Or guilty stuff like 'If I want to be a good mother, I shouldn't make her unhappy' and 'I want her to like me.' The worst of it was about my mothering and how I was parented.

"Now when I realize that she's asking for more than she can eat, I recognize that my Identity System is driving my storyline. I talk to Ellie about how to have a clean plate and that she can choose to have seconds. She was frustrated and upset the first few times. However, I didn't get uptight about it because I knew I was responding in a new and appropriate way. Now she likes to have a clean plate, and she feels important, like a big girl, because she can decide what she wants next.

"At work, I've stopped looking for another job. I see that my boss's inability to appreciate me is her issue. It's up to me if I make it my issue. When I feel that tug in my gut, I know my fixer and depressor are working me over. I do find it helpful to label the thoughts and listen to the background sounds. Usually I become less uptight, but even if I don't, I open up, carry on, and feel liberated. When my boss doesn't show me consideration or uses me as a gofer, I use that to be more aware of my Identity System's requirements and storylines. Rather than being an insult, it's an opportunity. In fact, I've discovered that whenever people are mean, it can be an opportunity. It can even be a blessing. However, more often than not it takes me time to detect the blessing!

"I've come to terms with the guilt I'd felt over my brother's drug usage. My Identity System was weaving storylines that I was somehow responsible, and yet I know that I'm not. I decided to do a map about Frank. Apart from the guilt-related items, there was my fixer, trying to fix him. If I don't fix him I feel bad, and that's where the guilt comes in. I can now see that my wanting to fix Frank is all about my own storylines. It has given me more breathing room. I've begun to work on a Decision map about what I can do, if anything, about Frank and his habit. The problem is creating less havoc for me. I have space to think about Frank and his problem without getting so upset, more space and quietness simply to be with him as he is and get to know him better without putting my storyline requirement blinders on. I'm feeling closer to him, and he seems to be a bit more comfortable with me. Even when I talk about things that are hard for him to hear, he seems to sense that I'm talking as a loving sister. I think that is because I am much more open with my new practice.

"There is something else: I try to do the bridging awareness practice for a couple of minutes when I start to eat. My appreciation of the food and myself is better then. Like last night, I wanted a snack, and rather than follow my pattern of chips, soda, and pie, I had an apple. I keep it in the refrigerator so it's cold. I take a minute to feel its smoothness, roundness, and coldness. It's fun. Next I slowly bite into it and sense the pop as my teeth puncture the skin. I sense the tartness and savor the crunchiness. One apple and some water is now satisfying. I used to eat on and on, unaware that I was full. Without any special diet, I've lost ten pounds—and I enjoy my meals more.

"I'm looking forward to making this practice work for me. It is 'work,' because it does need attention and care, but in a way, it's not. It's becoming so much more natural for me to bridge. Having thoughts is not such a big deal after all! I'm particularly interested in observing my storylines as they come up, to see if they help me to be present and aware, or if they box me into one of the Identity System's loops.

"If you asked me now what my problems are, I'd say my Identity System is my only problem. I even enjoy working on it. The more I do so, the more my other problems become manageable.

When you first spoke about the 'true self,' I didn't understand it at all. I still can't find words to describe it. My true self is like a 'no-self'—I mean, no fixed or limited self—because it is so spacious, vast, open, and ever changing. The best thing for me is that it is all about being present—right here, right now. I enjoy becoming more responsive and aware. It feels like home. I'm even beginning to welcome my fixer and depressor. They make sure that I know when I am not present and responsible. My life is definitely changing for the better."

David

David's need to excel and push himself was slowed; he learned to rely less on his wife and his boss's approval for his own happiness, and he has begun to savor life's small but exquisite pleasures:

"Others are responding to me differently. Anita is sweeter to me, we're closer, and our lovemaking is better. Whenever I see my fixer or depressor acting up, I just observe the thoughts. If I come home and Anita doesn't smile, I don't have to get tense and upset. It feels freer. I have choices. I'm not all tied up. When I drive to work, I feel open to sounds and vibrations and alert to what's happening, to my body's sensations. I noticed I'm not automatically listening to the radio anymore. I'm present with my driving.

"At work, when I'm doing paperwork, every half hour I come to my senses. I like the expression. I get to be sane and present. I just pause, label a few thoughts, and I'm more productive. Don't get me wrong: I still get upset when a deal doesn't work out or I think I've got on the wrong side of the boss. When I do get upset, I try to catch it by taking a few deep breaths and sensing how my body is reacting. It takes just a few seconds and it helps. Now I see it sooner and take care of it. I had a client on the telephone the other day who had a lot to say and was repeating himself. I started to doodle a map of what was on my mind. It let me know where I was. I saw how my feeling 'little' was stopping me from being more assertive. The call went well; I was ready, when he stopped talking, to be assertive, to pick up what was important to the deal and drop all my stuff, including my stuff about him. He's tedious, but I didn't let it get to me this time. Now I do these doodle maps more often, and they help me find my direction. I have choices. I don't have to be pulled by the Identity System, but I am free to go wherever, even if it is in the Identity System direction.

"What I see in my mapping is that the Identity System is a constant presence. When I am not aware, that constant pull leads me to experience and express the damaged self. The doodle maps give me freedom to open up, relax, and make choices. Of course, it does not mean that everything works out perfect—it doesn't. However, it's a good process. It's improving my quality of life and my effectiveness. When things go wrong, I'm not in crisis.

"Like Carla when she's eating, I just tune in more. When I'm on the treadmill, I pay attention to whatever's happening in my body rather than trying to escape mentally. I used to get through exercising by watching the clock or TV. I enjoy it more than ever, so naturally I work out more. I'm in a lot better shape. I'm not so revved up, and I'm not so oppressed by my thoughts and feelings. I used to be afraid of my thoughts. My family life is much better. I've noticed that when I have a few free moments, I don't try to fill them up. I feel good just to be aware. Of course, my Identity System wants to push me, but I just label the 'push.'

"I have been playing golf regularly since I was a teenager, but my handicap hasn't budged much over the past five years. Since I started bridging, I frequently tune in to the bird sounds, the far-away traffic noises, the smell of the freshly cut grass, the wind on my face, and I automatically become more aware of the sensations of my fingers on the club and my body movements. I'm not consciously trying to do anything new, but there is a better flow to my game, and my swing is relaxing. When I miss an easy putt or end up in the rough, I don't ruminate about it. If thoughts come up about the last stroke or hole, I label them and enjoy the day. My handicap has dropped four strokes over the past six weeks.

"Mapping and bridging are part of my life, but there are still times when I need to remind myself to do it. However, I'm finding that bridging is becoming quite natural and automatic, like when I'm brushing my teeth or taking a shower. It's helpful driving to and from work. My problems no longer overwhelm me. I work on them when I need to, and I'm making good progress. Before I began bridging, they were dominating my life. My Identity System's still around, but it's not driving me so much. I have more space. For instance, my main problem, 'I need more self-control,' was a bogus problem. It's like saying I need to fix my fixer. The more I controlled, the more restricted I became. Bridging enabled me to see that my Identity System was the real problem there. I began to see when my free thoughts of wanting to be in control were confiscated by the Identity System. I saw that whenever I thought I needed to control the situation, I became full of fear and bodily tensions. Once I opened my awareness to this, I saw that the idea of not being in control confirmed my sense of damage and limitation. The 'Peace of Mind' map showed me how dominant this requirement had become and how enmeshed it was in my physical, mental, and emotional patterns. By continuing to bridge whenever this comes up, I am now able to take charge of a situation at work without tension and fear, and I can see when to watch and wait. At home, I can be assertive with Jimmy but calm and collected. I'm less threatening and less distant with him, and we're connecting better."

Robert

Robert, a successful physician with a wonderful reputation for caring and service, rediscovered the absolute value of his own daughter, a value he had forgotten about in the face of disappointment with her actions. With mapping of his requirements and bridging, his compassion flowed as he gained a new appreciation for life in all its joys, disappointments, and challenges. He allowed his natural self to bring him the fullness of a full, non-polarized life.

His bridging journey began when his twenty-year-old unmarried daughter, Suzy, gave birth to a son. She lived with her boyfriend a while, tried living alone with the child, and then eventually came back home to "sort things out." Although Robert and his wife were attentive to their daughter and grandson's needs and he did his best to be kind and compassionate, a wall arose between himself and Suzy. He had trouble sleeping, began having headaches, let his exercise regimen stop, and became irritable. His behavior toward his daughter and his physical symptoms went hand in hand as his limited awareness became even more cramped by the requirements "I need to be caring toward Suzy" and "I need to be close to Suzy." Meanwhile, he had judged Suzy to be relatively less than a "good daughter" because of the challenging space she was in. His friends had children of the same age, many of whom were excelling in college or becoming financially independent, and he felt embarrassed by Suzy's situation.

When his fixer requirements were not fulfilled, Robert experienced himself as damaged. When his daughter was unhappy and the baby cranky, it confirmed that he was a bad father and grandfather. No matter how hard he tried to be a good father, his relationship with Suzy was strained. After a few sessions of bridging, he quickly started to see his requirements. He came to appreciate Suzy for who she was. He began sleeping more soundly and taking better care of himself.

Robert experienced a dramatic shift of perspective. With expanded awareness, he was able to naturally embrace his daughter's situation. His mind became more settled and his body more relaxed. After one of his bridging sessions, he came home, greeted everybody, and for the first time in years, he gave his daughter a heartfelt hug. He became tearful and said, "I love you." The barrier between him and Suzy melted, and his expanded awareness allowed him to both receive and give of his true self. Once he made this shift, he had a living knowledge about his wondrous natural self. This knowing naturally manifested in his doing.

Your Knowing Becomes a Doing
Becomes Your Life Transformed

You don't have to stay lost in your busy head and your damaged self. You have already begun to transform with a diligent awareness practice of bridging to your Source. As you continue to do so, you will experience a newfound calmness. Your relationships will improve along with your physical and mental health. All are signposts that your life is turning around. However, for your spiritual ship to turn—to have a true and long-lasting healing, a true peace of mind, and an imperturbable sense of well-being— you must see and experience your Source with your entire body-mind. Do this by resting your Identity System. It is blind to your true self, to your spiritual world. As you learn to rest it, you will experience the healing pouring out from the Source as you function in harmony and balance in your everyday life.

Different people move at different speeds. Do what you do. Just remember the components of bridging: coming back to your senses, recognizing your Identity System requirements, and resting them. When you do this consistently, you'll find yourself transformed, and you'll move into a new place where bridging becomes programmed into your very being. Once you have learned to ride a bicycle, you don't have to think of how to make the next turn, because your body, virtually at a cellular level, performs as required. So too will your body-mind react to life's stresses, bridging naturally and effortlessly each day through joys, problems, and challenges. When you rest your Identity System, your expanded awareness leads to a knowing, which in turn leads to a doing. On your bridging journey, you will know just what to do. Never forget that the magic doesn't reside in this book, in me, or with others but is always and forever within you.

What's your issue or problem? Chances are it has been discussed in this book! Use the list below to find discussions of how bridging and mapping can help you sort through various life issues. You'll also find specific stories of people for whom bridging their Identity System transformed their life, helping them to use their innate natural functioning to solve their problem or to simply lead a more satisfying life.

I n d e x

OTHER BOOKS FROM
BEYOND WORDS PUBLISHING, INC.

The Hidden Messages in Water
Author: Masaru Emoto
$16.95, softcover

Imagine if water could absorb feelings and emotions or be transformed by thoughts. Imagine if we could photograph the structure of water at the moment of freezing and from the image "read" a message about the water that is relevant to our own health and well-being on the planet. Imagine if we could show the direct consequences of destructive thoughts or, alternately, the thoughts of love and appreciation. *The Hidden Messages in Water* introduces readers to the revolutionary work of Japanese scientist Masaru Emoto, who discovered that molecules of water are affected by thoughts, words, and feelings. Dr. Emoto shares his realizations from his years of research and explains the profound implications on the healing of water, mankind, and earth.

The Power of Appreciation
The Key to a Vibrant Life
Authors: Noelle C. Nelson, Ph.D., and Jeannine Lemare Calaba, Psy.D.
$14.95, softcover

Research confirms that when people feel appreciation, good things happen to their minds, hearts, and bodies. But appreciation is much more than a feel-good mantra. It is an actual force, an energy that can be harnessed and used to transform our daily life—relationships, work, health and aging, finances, crises, and more. *The Power of Appreciation* will open your eyes to the fabulous rewards of conscious, proactive appreciation. Based on a five-step approach to developing an appreciative mind-set, this handbook for living healthier and happier also includes tips for overcoming resistance and roadblocks, research supporting the positive effects of appreciation, and guidelines for creating an Appreciators Group.

Water Crystal Oracle

Based on the work of Masaru Emoto, author of *The Hidden Messages in Water*

48 Water Crystal Cards, $ 16.95

Masaru Emoto, author of the best-selling book *The Hidden Messages in Water*, discovered that molecules of water can be affected by our thoughts, words, and feelings. When water is frozen, the crystals reveal the concentrated thoughts directed toward them. Included in *Water Crystal Oracle* are 48 beautiful water-crystal images to both enhance your life and balance your well-being in many ways.

Ocean Oracle

What Seashells Reveal about Our True Nature

Author: Michelle Hanson

$26.95, boxed set (softcover with card deck)

Combining the ancient art of divination with the mysticism of seashells and their interaction with humankind throughout time, *Ocean Oracle: What Seashells Reveal about Our True Nature* borrows from many disciplines to produce a new and inspiring divination system based on seashells. The boxed set is comprised of 200 full-color seashell cards, a companion book, and a four-color foldout sheet with overview plates of the 200 shells. Appreciation for the shells' aesthetic beauty is enhanced by the text descriptions detailing the animals' behaviors, abilities, interactions with humankind, and their meaning. The shells serve as tools to assist you in revealing subconscious, hidden beliefs and attitudes.

The Gifts of Change

Author: Nancy Christie

$14.95, softcover

The Gifts of Change explores the commonplace activities that are part and parcel of everyday life—an unwelcome gift, an unwanted rejection, an unexpected schedule disruption. Readers are invited to look beyond the surface of occurrence for hidden meanings and subtle truths. The result is a shift in their perceptions about themselves and the life they are living—and the choices they have.

When we welcome change, we find opportunities for growth and development. New strengths and hidden abilities become apparent to us. Life itself becomes an expansive and ever-expanding process. By embracing those changes that come into our lives, we are able to learn from them, ultimately creating a richer, deeper, more fulfilling life.

Live in the Moment

Author: Julie Clark Robinson
$13.95, softcover

Fresh, funny, and blatantly honest, *Live in the Moment* holds the secret to harnessing the power of the present. A practical book about creating one's own life experiences, author Julie Clark Robinson's words of inspiration will help you to create your own mental treasure chest. *Live in the Moment* is for those times when we simply need to stop allowing life's ups and downs to dictate how we feel and look to ourselves to set the tone. If you're willing to lighten up one minute, dig deep the next, and be painstakingly honest throughout, you will come away with a revitalized outlook on life.

To order or to request a catalog, contact
Beyond Words Publishing, Inc.
20827 N.W. Cornell Road, Suite 500
Hillsboro, OR 97124-9808
503-531-8700

You can also visit our Web site at *www.beyondword.com* or e-mail us at *info@beyondword.com*.

Beyond Words Publishing, Inc.

OUR CORPORATE MISSION
Inspire to Integrity

OUR DECLARED VALUES
We give to all of life as life has given us.
We honor all relationships.
Trust and stewardship are integral to fulfilling dreams.
Collaboration is essential to create miracles.
Creativity and aesthetics nourish the soul.
Unlimited thinking is fundamental.
Living your passion is vital.
Joy and humor open our hearts to growth.
It is important to remind ourselves of love.